THE ECONOMICS
OF HEINRICH PESCH

RICHARD E. MULCAHY, S.J.
UNIVERSITY OF SAN FRANCISCO

NEW YORK
HENRY HOLT AND COMPANY

To

    MY MOTHER

and

    THE MEMORY OF MY FATHER

PREFACE

Heinrich Pesch, though called the leading Catholic authority on economics, is almost unknown to Anglo-American economists. His social philosophy, solidarism, has received some limited recognition; his economic doctrine, buried in five heavy German tomes, has hardly been noticed. The primary purpose of this book is to present Pesch's relatively unexplored economic doctrine to the English-speaking world. A by-product may be a suitable text in welfare economics.

It was felt that the usefulness of this work could be enhanced if—when such a relation was significant—Pesch's doctrine was linked up with the pertinent Anglo-Saxon economic literature. At times this was necessary for either a new problem was raised by the German economist or an old problem was approached from a new aspect. By thus relating Pesch's doctrine with conventional theory it is hoped that perhaps both *termini* may have been enriched, and that this work may serve as a framework text for economic theory.

In general the conventional categories of economic theory have been followed. Consumption theory, however, frequently neglected or placed in the appendices, is given a prominent place. This exception follows from the normative character of economics, as viewed by Pesch, and the consequent teleological approach evident throughout his work. On the other hand, monetary theory has been placed in an appendix. This should not be interpreted as if either Heinrich Pesch or the author underestimates the importance of monetary theory. Pesch devoted 155 pages to the topic. It is merely that beyond a forceful mode of presentation he does not seem to make any contribution to theory here.

No doubt the reader will find a few other "surprises." For example, a paucity of criticism has been offered of Pesch's doctrine. Perhaps in defense of this singularity I may quote the words of Professor Vincent W. Bladen explaining his approach to his study of John Stuart Mill:

> I am not interested in looking down from the heights that we have since achieved to point out the inadequacies of the "founders." I am inclined to look back to see what we can still learn from them.[1]

For, despite his modernity, Pesch is in a true sense a "founder." He was the first economist to construct an economic theory on the foundation of Aristotelian-Thomistic philosophy. He considered it essential that an economic theory, and also the organizational principle of the economy be established on a sound social philosophy.

This fundamental approach has occasioned what probably will be another unexpected feature. A philosophic framework will be evident throughout the work. Actually this should not be too surprising for all economic theory has a philosophic foundation, whether it be explicit or, as is more common, implicit. Pesch made explicit his philosophic as-

---

[1] "John Stuart Mill's *Principles:* A Centenary Estimate," *American Economic Review,* XXXIX, Proceedings (May, 1949), p. 1.

sumptions, and without these his economic theory cannot be understood.

Some may be surprised that, though Pesch's work is called the source-book of the encyclical, *Quadragesimo Anno,* no references are made in this book to this or any other encyclical. A social encyclical is carefully prepared and strives to be scientifically accurate, but it makes no claim to be a technical treatise on economics. It may offer leads for the economic theorist; its purpose is, however, satisfied if it presents valid socio-philosophic principles to be implemented by the economist. The influence of Heinrich Pesch on the doctrine contained in *Quadragesimo Anno* is recognized by every scholar in the field, so that no useful service would have been performed by myriad references to the latter work. If I may paraphrase words used in a more sublime context, for those who accept the encyclicals no reference to them is needed, for those who do not accept them any reference would be useless. I chose instead to refer to the writings of economists, whose close agreement with Pesch the reader may not have anticipated.

Expressions of one's gratitude for the aid, encouragement, and criticism received in the preparation of a book are customary; on this account, however, neither the benefits received nor the appreciation of these benefits should be considered commonplace. My superiors in the Society of Jesus have been most generous in making it possible for me to spend the years of research and writing necessary to produce this work. In the organization and carrying out of this project Professor William J. Fellner of the University of California has been most generous with his time and judicious counsel. The late Professor Leo Rogin of the University of California encouraged me in this work and made many useful suggestions. Helpful assistance, general or specific, was given by Professors Sanford Mosk, Carl O. Sauer, and Howard S.

Ellis of the University of California; Professors Andrew
Boss, S.J., Arthur Falvey, S.J., George Lucy, S.J., and Fred-
eric Breier of the University of San Francisco; Professor Ed-
ward Chamberlin of Harvard University; Professor Jacques
Yenni, S.J., of Loyola University of New Orleans; Professor
Carl Benecke, S.J., of Loyola University of Los Angeles; and
Mr. F. P. Kenkel, Director of the Central Bureau of the
Catholic Central Verein of America.

Many European scholars, visited during a research trip to
Europe in 1949, gave me valuable assistance. The two internationally famous disciples of Heinrich Pesch, Professors
Gustav Gundlach, S.J., of the Gregorian University in Rome
and Oswald von Nell-Breuning, S.J., of Sankt Georgen in
Frankfurt were especially helpful. Professors Lionel Robbins
of the London School of Economics, Mr. R. G. Hawtrey of
the British Treasury, and Professor R. F. Harrod of Christ
Church, Oxford, kindly discussed with me the fundamental
question of the nature of economic science.

It is obvious that a study of a man who wrote as much as
Heinrich Pesch could hardly be carried out without the co-
operation of many helpful librarians. Particularly generous
have been the librarians of the University of San Francisco,
the University of California, the Gregorian University of
Rome, Sankt Georgen in Frankfurt, and the public library
in München-Gladbach. On a rainy afternoon in the base-
ment of this public library my search for all the writings of
Heinrich Pesch came to an end. By means of the library con-
fiscated by the National Socialist Party from the Volksverein
(when they were suppressed in 1934) and now stored in the
München-Gladbach public library, Pesch's works not found
elsewhere, were discovered. A complete list of Pesch's writings will be found in the bibliography.

Chapter II on the nature of economic science, except for
the section on the goal of the economy and some minor

changes, appeared in *The Quarterly Journal of Economics* of August, 1949 as "The Welfare Economics of Heinrich Pesch." The Pesch bibliography and an article entitled "Economic Freedom in Pesch" appeared in the April, 1951 issue of *Social Order*. The contents of this article are scattered through various chapters. I am grateful to the editors of these reviews for permission to reproduce this material here. For permission to use quotations, identified in the text, I am indebted to the editors and publishers of these works. Valuable secretarial assistance was rendered by Mrs. Dale Cuniffe, Miss Geraldine Guenter, and Miss Josefa Mapa. Miss Elsbeth Nagel helped read the proofs.

Richard E. Mulcahy, S.J.

University of San Francisco, California
December 8, 1951

CONTENTS

xi

CHAPTER ONE

INTRODUCTION

B ECAUSE Heinrich Pesch is comparatively little known to economists in the English speaking world, a few introductory remarks seem required. So, a brief sketch of the important events in Pesch's life and some general indications of his position in the broad stream of social and economic thought, particularly of his time, will be offered in this chapter. These background facts and views should prove helpful in the understanding and appreciation of his economic theory.

1. Heinrich Pesch

Heinrich Pesch, S.J., was born in Cologne on September 17, 1854, and died at Valkenburg, Holland, on April 1, 1926.[1] His

---

[1] The following biographical sketch is based for the most part on Pesch's autobiography in *Die Volkswirtschaftslehre der Gegenwart in Selbstdarstellungen*, F. Meiner (ed.) (Leipzig, 1924), Vol. 1, pp. 190–208. For references in English see the article, "Heinrich Pesch," by Goetz Briefs in the *Encyclopedia of the Social Sciences*, XII (1937), pp. 91–92; Franz Mueller's brochure, *Hein-*

first social studies were made at the University of Bonn in 1872, at which time his professor of economics was Erwin Nasse. On January 10, 1876, he entered the Society of Jesus and was trained during the next fourteen years in classical literature, philosophy, theology, higher mathematics, and the natural sciences. The four of these years of study spent in England gave him a realization of the distressed lot of the Lancashire workingman, one of the main motives inspiring him to dedicate his life to the aid of the laboring classes. He was ordained to the priesthood in 1888. His first article, "Zinsgrund und Zinsgrenze," [2] appeared the same year.

After the completion of the formal course of the Jesuit Order, Pesch devoted himself for the next ten years to the private study of economic theories and conditions. For a short while he was associated with the *Stimmen aus Maria-Laach* (later called *Stimmen der Zeit*), for which as a contributor over a period of thirty-five years he wrote more than a hundred articles on economic and social questions. In 1890 at the invitation of Count Silva-Tarouca, later the last Minister of Agriculture of the Austrian Empire, Pesch stayed at Türmitz in North Bohemia. The socialist, Rudolph Meyer, was lecturing there. But, when Meyer, not able to answer Pesch's objections to the labor theory of value, took it as a personal affront, Pesch left for Vienna.[3] At Türmitz he had already begun his

---

rich Pesch and His Theory of Solidarism (St. Paul, 1941), and his article, "I Knew Heinrich Pesch," *Social Order* I (April, 1951), pp. 147–52. This particular issue of *Social Order* is devoted entirely to Heinrich Pesch in commemoration of the twenty-fifth anniversary of his death.

[2] *Zeitschrift für katholische Theologie*, XII (Heft 1, 3), pp. 36–74, 393–418.

[3] Heinrich Pesch, *Volkswirtschaftslehre der Gegenwart* I, *op. cit.*, pp. 5–6. It is difficult to understand the prominence given by some to Pesch's contact with Meyer, as if this follower of Vogelsang had been particularly influential on the thought of Pesch. There is no external evidence to be found in his autobiography to indicate this, nor is there any internal evidence in the *Lehrbuch*. The few references to Meyer in the latter work are either inconsequential items, referring mainly to historical questions, or are a refutation of Meyer's position.

Die Soziale Befähigung der Kirche;[4] and in Vienna he made
a study which developed into *Die Wohltätigkeitsanstalten der
Christlichen Barmherzigkeit in Wien.*[5]
The next eight years found him in Mainz as spiritual director of the diocesan seminary. During this period his influence began to spread, and he came in contact with the German Catholic Center Party and the social-minded circles of
München-Gladbach, of the French "Semaines," and Rheims.
And, while living in the house in which the great social bishop,
von Kettler, had lived and worked, he wrote his fundamental
two-volume work, *Liberalismus, Sozialismus und christliche
Gesellschaftsordnung.*[6]

In 1901, at the age of forty-seven, he resumed the formal
study of economics, to investigate the latest scientific developments, particularly the contributions of the so-called "ethical"
school. After considering and rejecting London, Paris, and
Vienna, he chose Berlin, the center at the time of the most
famous German economists. For two years he studied at the
University of Berlin under Gustav Schmoller, Max Sering,
and the professor to whom he attached himself most closely,
Adolph Wagner.

From then until his death, twenty-three years later, Pesch
was devoted to his monumental life-work, *Lehrbuch der Nationalökonomie.*[7] He established residence at the Jesuit House
of Writers in Luxemburg, where he was delighted to have at
his disposal all the important economic literature from England, America, France, Austria, Switzerland, and Germany.
The journal literature was particularly esteemed, for, as he
said, "the science makes its progress in the journals."[8] In 1905
appeared the first volume of the *Lehrbuch.* But the strenuous

---

[4] (Berlin: Germania, 1893; 3rd ed.; 1911.)
[5] (Freiburg i. Br.: Herder, 1891.)
[6] (Freiburg i. Br.; Herder, 1896–99; 2nd ed.; 1901.)
[7] 5 vols. (Freiburg i. Br.; Herder, 1905–23; vols. I–III, 2nd–6th ed.; 1924–26).
[8] Heinrich Pesch, *Volkswirtschaftslehre der Gegenwart* I, *op. cit.*, p. 8.

effort to cover all pertinent literature and digest it had taken
its toll and he fell seriously ill. He admitted later that even in
his sleep he had not been able to forget his work, and if he
awakened and recalled a clear formula which came to him he
would spring out of bed to jot it down. For awhile, the doc-
tors despaired for his life, but after the inactivity of a year, he
resumed his work. The second volume appeared in 1909.

The following year he moved to Berlin Marienfelde, where
for fifteen years, while continuing the *Lehrbuch,* he undertook
the spiritual direction of the unfortunate girls in the care of
the Good Shepherd Sisters. During World War I his most
important journal article appeared, "Volkswirtschaftliche Aufgabe und Weltwirtschaft." [9] In 1918 was published *Ethik und
Volkswirtschaft,* which stressed the importance of ethical standards in economic life.[10] And in the troubled transition postwar days he wrote four popular pamphlets contrasting his solidaristic system of labor with individualistic capitalism and
socialism: *Nicht kommunistischer, sondern christlicher Sozialismus;* [11] *Sozialisierung;* [12] *Neubau der Gesellschaft;* [13]
Christlicher Solidarismus und soziales Arbeitssystem.[14]

After many interruptions due to his continual ill-health the
fifth and last volume of the *Lehrbuch* appeared in 1923. Except for revised editions, this completed the monumental
work, which now covered almost four thousand pages. New
editions were demanded more quickly than he was able to produce them. Honorary degrees were bestowed on him in the
closing years of his life by the University of Cologne and the
University of Münster. Pesch's life was dedicated to research
and writing; according to K. E. Nickel, he "twice received an

9 *Weltwirtschaftliches Archiv,* VI, 2nd h. (Heft 1, 1915), pp. 21–40.
10 (Freiburg i. Br.: Herder, 1918.)
11 (Berlin: Deutsche Zentrumspartei, 1918.)
12 (Freiburg i. Br.: Herder, 1919.)
13 (Freiburg i. Br.: Herder, 1919.)
14 (Berlin: Deutsche Zentrumspartei, 1919.)

invitation to foreign universities, but declined them because his work was still uncompleted." [15]

Throughout his life Pesch manifested a sincere devotion to and esteem of the science of economics. His favorite reference to economics was the familiar "our science." [16] His objective attitude and charity in dealing with his colleagues is worthy of quote:

> For me, useless and, particularly, personal spiteful controversies have always gone against the grain. Therefore in all five volumes of the *Lehrbuch* I have placed special emphasis on this: not to hurt a colleague even by a single word. One can indeed learn something from almost every scholar, and should not forget that his own system has not been raised above all criticism.[17]

2. His Place

It is not a simple task to establish Pesch in the economic and social thought of his time, and in the broader historical stream, because his doctrine is so varied in its levels of analysis, and so extensive in the subjects treated, and primarily because his doctrine overlaps that of many diverse groups. The clearest is perhaps the negative position of opposition to economic liberalism. Here he was a part of the strong reaction which had arisen in the nineteenth century against the social evils of a *laissez-faire*, market economy.[18] In this negative sense Pesch's fellows included such disparate figures as Marx, Say, Owen, Gide, Schmoller, Adolph Wagner, Vogelsang, Kautsky, and

---

[15] "Literaturberichte," *Volkswirtschaftliche Blätter*, XXVIII (Heft 1, 1929), p. 55.

[16] Heinrich Pesch, *Volkswirtschaftslehre der Gegenwart* I, *op. cit.*, p. 16.

[17] *Ibid.*

[18] See Karl Polanyi, *The Great Transformation* (New York: Rinehart, 1944), *passim*.

Hitze. All were agreed that an unregulated market could not solve the social problem, but in most cases this ended the area of agreement. Though this negative aspect is important as a partial explanation of Pesch's motivation and approach, his positive position is more significant.

One of the main characteristics of Pesch's work is its scholastic socio-philosophic foundation. These social principles developed in the Middle Ages by the scholastic philosophers, particularly by Thomas Aquinas, today form the philosophic foundation of all scientific Catholic social treatises. What is notable here is that Pesch is the first theorist who constructed an integrated economic theory based on Aristotelian-Thomistic philosophy. Because of this, he is sometimes referred to as the leading Catholic economist, which is correct only insofar as the scholastic philosophy is commonly held by Catholics; but its adherents are not limited to Catholics, for it is a philosophic system based on reason rather than faith.[19] Pesch touches this very point: "Catholicism gives to the world no economic system, it is committed to no definite economic position, is tied to no particular economic system" (III, 547).[20] And elsewhere he explains:

> If occasionally today the expression "christian" or "Catholic" economics is used, this can be misunderstood. Economics is a *natural* discipline, it has to do with a natural ordering of economic life, therefore with "natural ethics" (III, 61, note 3; italics in original).

He claims explicitly that in his work he has not "treated economic matters in a theological manner" (II, vi). Furthermore it is his belief that though his social philosophic system,

[19] Nor have all Catholic social scientists drawn the same conclusions from their common philosophic foundation. For example, the paternalistic system of the Catholic Le Play was not acceptable to Pesch.

[20] This and subsequent references embodied in the text are to the latest editions of the *Lehrbuch der Nationalökonomie*. The translations from the German have been made by the author.

solidarism, obtains its complete meaning from a Christian *Weltanschauung,* nevertheless it can be accepted by all from the standpoint of pure humanitarianism and the national welfare.

In the philosophic sense of "Catholic," Pesch may be called the first "Catholic" to write a complete scientific economic treatise.[21] The basis for this title is that in the Middle Ages economic problems were analyzed from the ethical point of view; any economic contributions were by-products of the scholastics' main interest. Moreover, even after economics became a distinct science—whether one wishes to say this dates from the Mercantilists or the Physiocrats—only fragmentary, specialized economic monographs, or only the social philosophic principles unintegrated with the new science were contributed by Catholics.[22]

Numerous are Pesch's immediate Catholic predecessors in the field of economics and its wider social framework. To Professor Joseph Ritter von Buss of the University of Freiburg in Breisgau, should probably go the title of the first in the line of the German Catholic social movement. Influential authors prior to him, however, were the Romanticists, Friedrich von Schlegel, Adam Müller, and Franz von Baader. Contemporaries of Buss were Adolph Kolping in the active field and Bishop Wilhelm von Kettler, prominent for his social action and writings. The chief characteristic of this period was the opposition to economic liberalism.

[21] Cf. Oswald v. Nell-Breuning, *Reorganization of Social Economy,* B. W. Dempsey (ed.) (New York: Bruce, 1936), p. 5, footnote 2: "Pesch is the only systematic Catholic writer whose work has received recognition as a scientific achievement from the general economic world." This footnote does not appear in the original German edition.

[22] Cf. Heinrich Lechtape, "Heinrich Pesch," *Staatslexikon,* IV (1931), col. 132: "Already for decades before Pesch a series of Catholic economists and social philosophers—from Vogelsang and Kettler to Hitze and Hertling—treated social and economic questions in numerous isolated studies. But the impregnation of these problems with all the tools of modern economic science and the construction of a complete system is the abiding service rendered by Pesch."

Around 1870 the German Catholic social movement was concerned not only with individualistic capitalism but also the rising socialist movement. The nineties were dominated by Hitze who sought the remedy for the social evils in the given social order, by Pieper who looked to the reconstruction of a new order, and by Georg von Hertling who sought a middle way between individualism and collectivism.[23]

In relation to the most famous Catholic social documents, the encyclicals, *Rerum Novarum* and *Quadragesimo Anno*, it can well be said that Pesch is the connecting link between them. He may be viewed as a commentator on *Rerum Novarum* of 1891 and the sourcebook of *Quadragesimo Anno* of 1931. Almost every contribution of the latter encyclical may be found in Pesch, while there is nothing in his work that is not consistent with the encyclical. This is not surprising for Pesch had analyzed and synthesized the contributions of his fellow Catholic social scientists.

In the general history of social thought Pesch stands as the leading proponent of solidarism, which stresses the concept of the "group." Solidarism's opposition to individualism, and the kind of capitalism based on it, is recognized; but at times the dissimilarity between solidarism and the systems which overemphasize the "whole," socialism, state socialism, and universalism, is not appreciated.[24] In socialism society becomes one homogeneous mass, and the economy the sole economic entity. State socialism, particularly of the Adolph Wagner variety, is based on the false philosophy that the sole title to ownership of property resides in the state, and the private possessor of property in the administration of his property is merely an officer of the state. This easily leads to an exagger-

---

[23] For a brief description of the work of these men see Hermann Sacher, "Schrifttum zur christlichen Gesellschaftslehre und zur Sozialen Frage," *Wörterbuch der Politik*, III: *Zur Sozialen Frage* (1949), cols. 210–12; and Goetz Briefs, "Pesch and His Contemporaries," *Social Order* I (April, 1951), p. 158.

[24] A fuller discussion of solidarism and socialism will be found in Chap. VII.

ated form of state interventionism. Universalism, beginning from the whole, conceives the individual only as part of this whole, and rejects the idea of people combining. On the other hand, Peschian solidarism considers society not as something that is "one" but as something that possesses "unity." Private property is presupposed; and private enterprise is conceived as an important constituent of the economy as a whole. It proposes to reconstruct the social order by the establishment of "groups" which will be self-governing economic bodies. It thus adds to the social order a middle entity between the individual and the state, while insisting on the rights and duties of both the individual and the state.

Nor does the name "solidarism" cover a homogeneous series of systems. Particularly in France, at the turn of the century solidarism was a popular slogan, and many groups seized upon the word as a banner to be raised aloft. Pesch offers a general critique of these various forms of solidarism, especially of the French variety, which clarifies the difference between them and his own:

> . . . there is no longer any doubt how solidarism in our sense is essentially distinguished from that series of systems which up to the present has claimed the name "solidarism." Without depreciating the abundant and worthwhile material for thought, which particularly the French solidaristic teaching offers, we must regret that not a few of these French scientists were always so strongly influenced by utilitarian, positivistic, evolutionistic, socialistic theories, by a forced biological analogy, or an untenable (empirical in appearance but in reality, aprioristic) sociology that it was impossible to lead followers to solidarism. Especially, from Gide's solidarism and similar forms our system is distinguished—prescinding from a fundamental difference of principles—particularly in that we do not place the co-operative society and especially that of the consumer one-sidedly in the foreground, but assert the whole regulative and constructive significance of the solidaristic prin-

ciple for the ordering and shaping of that part of the politico-social life which we called the national economy (I, 444).

An important feature of Peschian solidarism is that the emphasis is not on the institutional framework, though the vocational groups are considered an essential of the system; the vital factor is the "spirit" motivating the men organized in these institutions. It is recognized that without the proper motivation the vocational group organization can be harmful for the nation. The proper spirit is the acknowledgment of the welfare of the whole as the goal of the economic strivings of the individuals.

Today the leading representatives of the solidaristic school are Gustav Gundlach, S.J., professor in the Gregorian University, Rome; Oswald von Nell-Breuning, S.J., a professor in St. Georgen Hochschule, Frankfurt; Professors Goetz Briefs of Georgetown University, Washington, D.C., and Heinrich Rommen and Franz Muller of St. Thomas College, St. Paul.

How should Pesch be classified as an economist in the technical sense of the word? In general, he is a welfare economist in contradistinction to the proponents of "pure" economics. And he is a teleological welfare economist in distinction to the modern positivistic welfare group. In doctrine and approach he is closer to Smith and Malthus than to Ricardo; to Sismondi than Say; Marshall than Robbins or Hicks; Keynes than Pigou.

What characterizes his work as an economist? Or, what contribution has Pesch to offer economic thought? He offers a sound philosophic foundation for many fundamental concepts and principles of economics. A fully developed analysis of the nature of the economy and economic science is found in his work. In particular the normative character of economic science is firmly established upon the concept of the goal of the economy. Moreover, criteria for policy drawn from this goal and applicable to the various segments of the economic process (e.g., consumption, production, distribution) have been developed.

Other examples of the value of Pesch's philosophic approach may be seen in the light it throws on certain principles and maxims of conventional theory. It is particularly evident in price theory where the innovation of monopolistic competition has shaken a naive acceptance of the competitive model as an optimum.[25] Also in the study of comparative economic systems the problem of the reconciliation of the interest of the individual and the community finds a satisfactory solution in the Peschian social system of labor. And because his system is not limited to the mathematically measurable, Pesch is able to introduce into his analysis intangible factors. Thus in the study of the organization of the economy the psychological factor of the "spirit" motivating the economy is given a prominent place.

Another characteristic of Pesch's work is his eclecticism. What makes it worthy of note is not so much that the truth has been sought wherever it might be found—whether in the writings of Karl Marx, Adam Smith, Adolph Wagner, or Alfred Marshall—but that these diverse thoughts are so agreeably harmonized. It is one thing to select the best from the works of only one school of thought, it is much more difficult to choose truths from authors with fundamentally different approaches and to harmonize these apparent contradictories

[25] Cf. E. H. Chamberlin, "Product Heterogeneity and Public Policy," *American Economic Review*, XL, Proceedings (May, 1950), p. 92: ". . . the consequences of product heterogeneity for welfare economics have been either ignored or seriously misunderstood. Monopoly elements are built into the economic system and the ideal necessarily involves them. Thus wherever there is a demand for diversity of product, pure competition turns out to be not the ideal but a departure from it. Marginal cost pricing no longer holds as a principle of welfare economics (not even for toll bridges); nor is the minimum point on the cost curve for the firm to be associated with the ideal. . . . What has been called the 'new welfare economics,' instead of being on a 'secure basis' as suggested by Professor Hicks, has quite misconceived a whole set of major problems. It is badly in need of a general overhauling."

in a consistent, workable system. This achievement is manifest in Pesch's reconciliation of the objective and subjective approach in value theory, and the reconciliation of the role of the individual and society in the economic system.

In evaluating Pesch's work it must be borne in mind that he is a pioneer.[26] He was satisfied to break ground, to advance theory along untraveled paths on which, because of their restricted concept of economic science, many economists did not dare to venture. The role of pioneer made Pesch aware that his work was not definitive, in the sense that further developments along the lines of his approach would be no longer possible. In his own words: "It would be presumptuous to assume that we have found the last, best, incontestable solution for the many questions of the modern economy" (IV, 19).

[26] At first sight this may seem to contradict Goetz Briefs' view that Pesch "enjoyed the privileges of a latecomer" and "wrote in the 'fulness of time' of Catholic social thought" ("Pesch and His Contemporaries," *op. cit.*, p. 160). But Pesch the "pioneer" and Pesch the "late-comer" are not necessarily contradictories. He came late into the field of Catholic social thought; he was a pioneer in constructing an economic system based on this social philosophy.

CHAPTER TWO

THE NATURE OF ECONOMIC SCIENCE

THE central issue emerging in this chapter is the question of whether the economy has a goal beyond the market-place aims of individuals. The problem arises from the primary purpose of this section, which is to present the nature of economic science according to Heinrich Pesch. To Pesch the nature of economics follows logically from the nature of the economic system. To what extent his position conforms with prevailing views will be indicated by reference to the recent Anglo-American literature on this topic.

Adam Smith's classical title, *An Inquiry into the Nature and Causes of the Wealth of Nations,* epitomizes the general approach of Pesch to the study of economics. His concern is the general welfare rather than private profit. He thus defines economics: "The science of the economic life (the process of providing material goods) of a people, considered as a social unit, bound together by the politico-social community life." Or, with direct application to the modern economy: "The science of the economic life of a politically united community,

13

on the level of a developed exchange economy, in relation to the national material welfare as a goal required by the social purpose of the political society" (I, 467).

1. A Goal to Be Attained

Before discussing the problem of the goal of the economy, it should be noted that Pesch, in agreement with most contemporary economists, holds that economics is a science. There is not, however, general agreement about what is meant by "a science." As Pesch points out, the dispute about the nature of economic science, which was a matter of intense interest in Germany at the turn of the century, is only a derivative of the more comprehensive battle in regard to the nature and method of science in general.[1] For him a science in the objective sense is "a summary of the general and certain knowledge and truths extending ultimately to the relatively last cause about a given subject" (I, 461). Some today would rather limit the notion to knowledge acquired by a particular method, such as *a priori* deduction, or to what can be measured, or can be verified by empirical tests.[2] In many respects the Peschian concept of economics is closer to the thought of those who deny economics is a science than it is to the position of some who

[1] Heinrich Pesch, "Eine neue Richtung in der Nationalökonomie," *Stimmen aus Maria-Laach*, LXXX (January, 1911), p. 54. For an outstanding exposition of the philosophic fundamentals involved here, see Gustav Gundlach, S.J., "Solidarist Economics," *Social Order*, I (April, 1951), pp. 181–85.

[2] For an example of the limited concept of science, see Lionel Robbins, *An Essay on the Nature and Significance of Economic Science* (2nd ed.; London: Macmillan, 1948), esp. pp. 104–106, 139–41; also his articles, "Live and Dead Issues in the Methodology of Economics," *Economica*, new series, V (August, 1938), p. 347; and "Interpersonal Comparisons of Utility," *Economic Journal*, XLVIII (December, 1938), p. 639. For a criticism of Robbins in conformity with Pesch's position, see Lindley Fraser, *Economic Thought and Language: A Critique of Some Fundamental Economic Concepts* (London: Black, 1947), pp. 30–31; and his article, "How Do We Want Economists to Behave?" *Economic Journal*, XLII (December, 1932), p. 560.

claim the prerogative of a science for economics but attempt to confine it within the narrow borders of the exact sciences.[3]

The social aspect of economics, which is not a matter of dispute among contemporary economists on the formal level of definition, receives particular emphasis in Pesch. For him, economics is not merely a theory of goods. Goods are needed, produced, exchanged, and consumed by men, who are not Robinson Crusoes, but who live in society. Moreover, as economics treats of the national whole, it deals with the economy of a politically united people. Still, he admits it is indisputable that "economic life has its source in human needs which are specific data existing for their own sakes independent of determined and particular social supposits and which clamor for satisfaction in every form of social organization" (I, 502).

The important conclusion which Pesch draws from the social aspect of economics marks the chief difference between the German economist and many modern theorists. It is that economics, being a social science, is concerned with a goal to be attained: "In the natural sciences it is a question only of the knowledge of causes and effects; in the social sciences, however, to which economics belongs the concern is ultimately about the knowledge of means and results in relation to a desired goal." [4] And in the *Lehrbuch* he adds the thought that the human conduct and striving, which are the object of research in a social science, are evaluated according to their adaptation to the purposes which they serve (I, 473–74).

The goal of the economy is the central notion of Pesch's

---

[3] See Frank H. Knight: "If we accept the aphorism, 'science is measurement,' as a definition of science, which is its only intelligible meaning, then there is no such thing as 'economic' science . . ." ("The Nature of Economic Science in Some Recent Discussion," *American Economic Review*, XXIV [June, 1934], p. 236). Raymond T. Bye: ". . . Science may almost be said to begin with measurement. . . . It is better, for the present, to designate economics as 'a branch of learning' than as a science" ("The Scope and Definition of Economics," *Journal of Political Economy*, XLVII [October, 1939], pp. 637–40).

[4] Heinrich Pesch, *Ethik und Volkswirtschaft, op. cit.*, p. 154.

concept of economic science. This means that "for the complete and correct establishment of the content of economic theory, the teleological method is of outstanding importance" (I, 565). For without first establishing the goal of the economy, there is no criterion of choice between the multitude of ends and means which confront the economist. "The choice of the means awaits . . . the determination of the goal" (*ibid.*). It is this goal which is used as the yardstick to determine which means are favorable, efficacious, or useful. The activities of individuals and organizations, and the production and distribution of goods, are called economically useful inasmuch as they serve this goal, and only insofar as they serve it.

The antithesis of the Peschian teleological position is to be found in the dictum of Lionel Robbins: "There are no economic ends." [5] It is claimed that "economics is entirely neutral between ends; that is, insofar as the achievement of *any* end is dependent on scarce means it is germane to the preoccupations of the economist." [6] If the dictum, "there are no economic ends," is only a cryptic way of saying that without the aid of some other discipline the economist cannot establish the goal of the economy, then, although the words are not happily chosen, there would be no disagreement in thought. If, however, this means that no matter what end is sought, whether to build a house or to live a life of debauchery, whether to produce "guns" or "butter," as long as it is done in an efficient way, it is economics—and this is apparently what Professor Robbins has in mind—then there is a most fundamental difference between Robbins and Pesch. The former considers only the economical use of the means; in fact, one wonders whether it would be a caricature of his position to portray it as "the means justifies the end." [7] Pesch, while giving due weight to

[5] Lionel Robbins, *Nature and Significance of Economic Science, op. cit.,* p. 145.
[6] *Ibid.,* p. 24. (Italics in original.)
[7] Cf. Howard S. Ellis, "The Economic Way of Thinking," *American Economic*

the economical application of means, sets up a higher criterion, the purpose for which the means are used economically. The issue has been put most aptly by his follower, Oswald von Nell-Breuning:

> Is there a *raison d'être* for the economy? In other words, has the economy as a whole, as a material phase of human social life, a material goal? Or does just each individual act in isolation, and does it depend only on him which goal he sets up in his economic activity? . . . The question aims much more at this, whether only that is true which daily experience teaches us, or whether *beyond* the different goals which individuals choose and *antecedent* to men setting up such material goals in their economic activity, does there simply pre-exist a *given material goal of the economy?* This would mean: all activities serving this objective, and producing fruits conducive to it, are exactly *on this account* "economic"; and whatsoever has nothing to do with this objective, has *exactly for this reason* nothing to do with the economy. All activities aiming at this objective, but producing untoward results, are again on exactly these grounds truly "economic," but wrongly applied.[8]

Even from the point of view of efficiency, recognition of the goal of the economy is important, for it is no less wasteful to be "economical" in the pursuit of a false objective than it is to

---

Review, XL (March, 1950), p. 3: "I differ significantly from the description given by Lionel Robbins that economics deals with the application of scarce resources to *given* ends. Robbins' description would, for example, include the analysis of productive effort to serve the ends given arbitrarily—and let us say for the present purpose, whimsically and sadistically—by an absolute dictator. But this is not economics. . . . Alternatively, one may express the same idea by saying that Robbins' definition errs in accepting any and all 'given ends'; one end must be stipulated by economics itself. . . ." (Italics in original.) Ellis' and the Peschian position agree on their criticism of Robbins' definition; they do not agree on what is the end of the economy.

[8] Oswald v. Nell-Breuning, *Die soziale Enzyklika* (Cologne: Katholische Tat-Verlag, 1932), pp. 61–62. (Italics in original.) In general I have followed the English translation of this passage offered in *Reorganization of Social Economy,* B. W. Dempsey (ed.), *op. cit.,* pp. 84–85, except where I have believed that a more literal translation would help to bring out the emphasis in the original.

be uneconomical while seeking the proper objective. As Cannan indicated in his criticism of Robbins, logically he should have no objection to a man burning down his house to cheat the insurance company, as long as he does not "use more matches than are necessary!" [9]

Heinrich Pesch does not ignore the idea of the efficient use of means. But he does hold that the principle of economy is broader than economics; it is a principle of reason applicable to all phases of human activity. "The 'principle of economy' (the optimum proportionality between means and ends, the greatest gain with the least effort) is a general principle of practical reason; a principle of prudent, rational management of affairs, proper not merely to economic life, but extending even to being a cosmic principle" (I, 467).[10] But, while economical choice of means is an indispensable condition and cause of most favorable results in economic activity, it still cannot be in itself a final determinant. It is subject to the correct ordering of ends. Technically the question is: what is being maximized?

[9] Edwin Cannan in his review of *An Essay on the Nature and Significance of Economic Science, Economic Journal*, XLII (September, 1932), p. 425.

[10] In an unsympathetic criticism of Pesch, Abram L. Harris charges "in no place does he completely grasp the notion of economy in its correct meaning of a rational allocation of scarce resources, which constitute a system of means for the satisfaction of wants, the latter being organized into a system of ends." And he accuses him of a "defective or wrong formulation of principle" in his view of economy ("The Scholastic Revival: The Economics of Heinrich Pesch," *Journal of Political Economy*, LIV [February, 1946], p. 41).

Minor defects in Mr. Harris' criticism of Pesch are that he makes use only of the first edition of the *Lehrbuch* I, published in 1905, rather than the latest revised edition of 1924; there is an illogical misinterpretation of Pesch's meaning in at least one sentence quoted; and statements of the principle of economy in a form in keeping with his own are overlooked, for example, in Volume IV, pp. 14, 133, 315. But the main weakness is that it seems unfair to accuse Pesch of a defective or wrong formulation because he does not always use a form whose acceptance is not undisputed among contemporary economists. Even Professor Frank H. Knight, the authority to whom Mr. Harris appeals, admits: " 'Cost,' in this sense (in the Marshallian boy-and-berries case) is 'pain cost,' or 'opportunity cost,' as one prefers; there is no real difference in meaning between the two" (*Risk, Uncertainty, and Profit* [Boston: Houghton Mifflin, 1921], p. 73).

Moreover, Pesch sees in the principle of economy itself an implicit teleological principle. The *homo economicus,* who seeks his greatest profit with the least sacrifice, is guided by a goal. He has a very clear idea of what wealth is, and he directs all his efforts toward the end which lies within this concept (I, 469). It is on similar grounds that Lindley M. Fraser has criticized Robbins:

> If he (Robbins) admits—as he clearly does—that it is an *objection* to a given way of achieving a purpose that it is "uneconomical," then he is implying that "economy" is an end and that waste is bad. He is assuming that "rational," i.e., economical choice is something worth striving for, and that this end is something with which the economist is directly concerned, and towards which he cannot be indifferent.[11]

Robbins' position that there are no economic ends seems to be the more common opinion today; it is always assumed at the textbook level, and many theorists, omitting all discussion, take it for granted. On the other hand, there are a large number of economists who have explicitly expressed the importance of the study of the goal of the economy. The latter group includes such names as J. M. Clark, Bye, Hawtrey, Wolfe, F. D. Graham, Salz, Walker, Suranyi-Unger, and the members of the American Economic Association committee on the Teaching of Undergraduate Economics.[12] To quote but

[11] "How Do We Want Economists to Behave?" *op. cit.,* p. 568. (Italics in original.)

[12] See J. M. Clark, "Some Current Cleavages Among Economists," *American Economic Review,* XXXVII, Proceedings (May, 1947), p. 9; Raymond T. Bye, "The Scope and Definition of Economics," *op. cit.,* p. 627; and his "Some Criteria of Social Economy," *American Economic Review,* XXXIV, Proceedings (March, 1944), pp. 1, 7–8; R. G. Hawtrey, "The Need for Faith," *Economic Journal,* LVI (September, 1946), pp. 363–64; A. B. Wolfe, "Economy and Democracy," *American Economic Review,* XXXIV (March, 1944), p. 3; Frank D. Graham (Discussion), "Ethics in the Study of Democratic Principles," *American Economic Review,* XXXIV, Proceedings (March, 1944), p. 55; Arthur Salz, "The Present Position of Economics," *American Economic Review,* XXXIV, Proceedings (March, 1944), pp. 18–19; E. Ronald Walker, *From Economic Theory to Policy* (Chicago: Chicago Press, 1943), *passim;* Theo Suranyi-Unger,

one of these, the American Economic Association committee reported:

> What economists study—in time series, for example—are categories of things which can only be created conceptually. Such categories require criteria, and criteria express value judgments. An economic system is not like the solar system, whose laws of motion call for no justification. As a system, an economy is more like a machine; "how it works" can be studied only if we posit some *end,* or *objective,* or value for which it— or some part of it—exists.[13]

It may be helpful to summarize here the main difference on the nature of economic science as between Pesch and the more conventional position represented by Robbins.

According to Pesch:	According to Robbins:
1. Economics is a social science, i.e., a summary of general truths of which we are certain.	1. Economics is a social science, i.e., a summary of truths derived from deduction, capable of being empirically tested.
2. The economy has a goal to be attained: the providing for the material needs of the people.	2. The economy has no goal.

"Facts and Ends in Economics," *Economic Journal,* XLIX (March, 1939), pp. 1–13; American Economic Association, "On Teaching Undergraduate Economics," *American Economic Review,* XL, Supplement (December, 1950), pp. 8–11.

It may be well to note that Bye in his "Scope and Definition of Economics," *op. cit.,* on p. 627, after attributing a function to be performed to the economy, denies that this is a teleological view, because "there is no implication that the social machinery of economizing has been consciously promoted by any beneficent creator, either human or divine, or that it accomplishes its task efficiently." This denial is based on an erroneous idea of the meaning of "teleological" and fails to appreciate that "function" in the sense of a task to be performed, and "teleological" are correlatives.

[13] *Op. cit.,* p. 11. (Italics added.)

According to Pesch (*cont.*):	According to Robbins (*cont.*):
3. In economics a teleological approach is required.	3. In economics a positivistic approach is sufficient.
4. The formal object of economic science is the goal of the economy.	4. The formal object of economic science is alternative choice.
5. The principle of economy is a subordinate criterion.	5. The principle of economy is the ultimate criterion.
6. Economic theory relies on social philosophy and ethics.	6. Economic theory is completely divorced from social philosophy and ethics.
7. Economics is a practical science.	7. Economics is a speculative science.
8. Economics is also a normative science.	8. Economics is only a positive science.

If we look for the fundamental reason for such a series of contradictory propositions, we will find it ultimately in the different concepts of "science" of the two authors. Robbins' skepticism has led him to consider scientific only that which can be measured, or which is subject to empirical test. This faulty epistemology coupled with the desire to build a purely scientific economics has led to his subsequent conclusions.

2. Objectivity of the Goal

If the goal of the economy is something more than the sum of individual market-place aims, how does the economist derive a knowledge of it? Is it sufficient to know what the opinion current in a given community at a given time postulates as the goal? Or, is it rather a question of an objective reality?

According to Pesch, unaided economic science cannot determine what is the aim of the economy. Nor is it sufficient to make an empirical study of current opinion, to take prevailing values as data. Knowledge of the goal of the economy is acquired by "philosophic deduction" from the notion and the nature of society and the economy (I, 532–33). Elsewhere he explains that after learning the supreme norm of all social theory from social philosophy, the economist draws the inferences required to achieve the aim of that part of social life which is called the national economy (I, 476).

Another objective feature of his concept of the aim of economic activity sets Pesch apart even from these economists who postulate a goal, to say nothing of the theorists who prescind from the question. In economic theory the most universally adopted position, when speaking about maximization and an optimum, is to refer to the maximization of the *satisfaction* of the consumer. Even when it is purged of all hedonistic elements, and is not a mere pain-pleasure analysis, the study of the process and term-product of the economy is always in terms of subjective satisfaction. This is evident from such statements as Harrod's, "The economic good is thus the preferred"; Hicks', "Each individual endeavoring to satisfy his tastes"; and Kaldor's, "How much (inequality) secures the maximum of total satisfaction." The subjective level of current theory was brought out most clearly when Professor Robbins, because of his dissatisfaction with satisfaction, popularized the debate on the correctness or incorrectness of interpersonal comparisons of satisfaction. This debate would not have taken place, or been deemed important, had it not been considered an essential assumption of economic theory that everyone has an equal capacity to derive satisfaction. Thus, Maine's Brahmin became of interest to economists because the consumption of goods was discussed in terms of a subjective "utility."

Like Adam Smith, Pesch conceives of economic activity as aiming at something objective, in a physical sense. It is not a question of pain and pleasure, or satisfaction in a psychological sense, but of providing for the material needs of the people.

> The physical and psychic enjoyment, attached to the satisfaction of a momentary want, cannot be the final goal of a struggle so severe and difficult which, for the most part, makes up the content of the lives of men (IV, 25–26).

> If we speak of providing for the needs of the people, it should not therefore be said that economic study must take the path of a psychology of subjective pain and pleasure. Considering the serious purpose of economic theory, that would be nothing more or less than a theoretical game. No, our study has in view not a pleasure sensation, but the question of the sufficient provision of the people, especially at its broader, lower levels, with good, fair-priced food, clothing, shelter, with all the material goods which they require for the satisfaction of their wants (I, 459).

However, the subjective element in economic activity is not overlooked by Pesch; it plays an essential part in motivation and is one of the elements in value theory. But even here the firm objective basis of a rational satisfaction is supposed:

> . . . evaluation does not rest on mere subjective "sensation," or subjective "feeling," but on the cognition of something objectively given. It is not an emotion, but a rational act, a judgment, a judgment of value. This judgment has as its object and its cause the objective usefulness of an economic good . . . (V, 73).

One main objection will certainly be raised against the position of Heinrich Pesch: how objective is the notion of material welfare?

Doubt as to the objectivity of the concept of material welfare arises because various schools seem to hold different views on what constitutes the material welfare of a nation. But this does not prove that the notion is something purely subjective.

> Rather it is a question of something very real which, I admit, in view of the diversity of subjects can acquire a peculiar, idealistic coloring in the minds of men according to their individual peculiarities. But, on this account, the goal by no means evaporates into the realm of a purely subjective ideal, rather it maintains its completely objective, real value, remains in the realm of objective truth, perceptible by rational cognition and capable of being scientifically established. There are available in reference to it positive and negative valuable criteria, and thus undoubtedly an extensive unity of opinion can be attained (I, 478–79).

If the concept of material welfare were purely subjective, then equally subjective would be the "common good" notion of the legal order, which would mean that political theory represents no reality, and that nothing remains but power politics.

Most, if not all, of the disagreement in this area concerns individual matters. But this is not a proof that the general notion is without meaning any more than the failure to agree about the income level at which a man may be classified as poor abolishes poverty.

Even the existence of different schools of social thought does not hinder the reaching of some sort of unanimity about the goal to be achieved. The Mercantilists, Physiocrats, and Adam Smith placed the welfare of the nation in the center of their theories, although they disagreed about how it was to be attained. At least, it should be possible to agree on a negative formulation. A contemporary example is the unanimous agreement that unemployment is an economic evil to be eliminated. And this negative approach can well be the bridge to the recognition of the positive requirements of national economic well-being.

3. The Goal of the Economy

What is the goal of the economy? On the whole the main body of modern economic theory has prescinded from the question. Notable exceptions are the writings of Harold Moulton, Raymond Bye, J. M. Clark, and E. Ronald Walker.[14] For Pesch the determination of the goal was crucial to the study of economics.

"Not material goods, nor their production, maintenance, increase, employment, nor the formation of wealth and capital, but the material welfare of men constitutes the aim of that aggregate of activities and institutions which are wont to be called the 'economy' . . ." (II, 297). "Welfare," a term widely used today in popular and scientific literature, refers in general to a condition or state of human well-being. Material welfare is defined as "welfare insofar as it arises from the suitable fullness of external, material, useful goods" (II, 287).[15]

The term material goods would have to include economic services. The specific use is found in Pesch: "The need is the need for external goods (material goods and economic services)" (IV, 29). The *rationale* of this is not without its problems, but it would probably be based on the relation of the service with some material good, such as servicing an automobile, performing housework, etc. These economic services

[14] See Harold Moulton, *Controlling Factors in Economic Development* (Washington, D.C.: Brookings, 1949), pp. 141–48; Raymond Bye, *Social Economy and the Price System* (New York: Macmillan, 1950), pp. 7–11; J. M. Clark, "Economic Means—To What Ends?" *American Economic Review,* XL, Supplement (December, 1950), pp. 37–42; E. Ronald Walker, *op. cit.,* pp. 228–45.

[15] This is the view also of Pigou who explains that economic welfare does not consist directly in "a man's income or possessions" ("Some Aspects of Welfare Economics," *American Economic Review,* XLI [June, 1951], p. 288). A certain subjectivism creeps into his view, however, when he further explains that welfare refers to a state of mind or consciousness, which is ultimately taken to mean satisfaction.

would be distinguished from educational, artistic, and similar services.

Although certain conceptual problems adhere to the division, it is essential to distinguish between material and immaterial or, if one wishes, between corporeal and spiritual welfare. Man's nature is composed of sensitive and rational elements, and likewise his welfare shares this duality. In practice material and immaterial welfare are frequently linked together. It may be that the same external good under different aspects can serve as well the bodily as the spiritual welfare of a man. For example, land offers a man by its fruit the necessary means to satisfy his need for food, clothing, and shelter; also it can offer him the possibility of self-expression, the opportunity to develop his personality, to satisfy his desire for ownership. But this does not destroy the essential distinction between the spiritual and material welfare—no more than the natural disposition of material goods to serve bodily needs is set aside because someone uses them in exchange to come into the possession of works of art.

Moreover, it is important for the science of economics to observe the distinction between material and immaterial welfare.

It is evident that within economic theory we have to do only with material welfare, at least insofar as it is a question of the immediate object of this science. Science, art, morality, jurisprudence, religion, etc., truly exercise the greatest influence on economic life. Also the actual realization of the spiritual welfare often depends on the use of material means. But everything which exerts an influence upon the economy or is dependent on it does not pertain to the object or within the sphere of economic theory. On the one hand, the distinction between material and spiritual welfare must be firmly maintained for the protection of the worth of man and the eminence of the spiritual-moral order; on the other hand, no less even in the interest of our science itself. That is to say, if this distinction is not observed, then either the whole life of the citizen must be reduced to the economic, or at least there is lacking a certain boundary between the economy and other spheres of human and political activities. At the same time, too, the sound point of view for the definition of important, fundamental economic notions is lost and the science itself is delivered up to an unstable vagueness. For example, what are economic goods, what is economic production and consumption, if economics includes all goods, if its scope rejects a clear circumscription? (II, 286–87).

Another crucial question in the determination of Pesch's thought is: in what sense is the welfare of all the people the goal of the economic system? "Is it the immediate well-being of the individual members, or is it a question here, first of all, of a social condition in which all the individual members participate?" (II, 297). The answer will be found only by resorting to social philosophy.[16] According to individualism which views society merely as an aggregate of isolated individuals, the national welfare is merely a sum of the welfare of the individuals.[17] Socialism, too, in a certain sense implies this concept of the welfare of the nation coupled with the assumption, however, that society is the responsible agent of this individual welfare. Pesch's solidaristic system rejects the one-sidedness of a mere aggregate concept of the economy and of a single economy controlled by society, and proposes an economic order and a moral-organic unity and community of many independent private economic units.

[16] A brief, but fuller explanation of these social philosophies will be found in Chapter VII.

[17] See Abram Bergson, "Socialist Economics," in *A Survey of Contemporary Economics,* Howard S. Ellis (ed.) (Philadelphia: Blakiston, 1948), pp. 417–18. Bergson offers a generalized Marshall-Pigou formula W F(U^1, U^2, U^3, ...), in which W is the welfare of the community, and U the utility of the individual household. He states that if a consumer sovereignty is supposed the welfare function may be expressed in this formula. It should be pointed out that Bergson rightly uses the term "may," for on the supposition of consumer sovereignty the welfare function may be expressed otherwise, as with Pesch.

According to the solidaristic approach "the goal of the economy" may refer either to: (1) the material side of the public welfare (*prosperitas publica*); or, (2) the general material welfare of the private enterprise (*prosperitas universalis*); or, (3) the prosperity of the nation, which embraces both the *prosperitas publica* and the *prosperitas universalis* (II, 298–99).[18] The material side of the public welfare is a public condition or state, and is the immediate object of the economy and of economic theory. It does not immediately secure for the individuals their own personal well-being, but provides the social environment, the possibility to attain it by their own efforts.[19] The general material welfare of the individual members is the total of the private material welfares. These two concepts, public and general welfare, are complementary. "Without the 'public' welfare, there is no permanent, secure 'general' welfare; but without a relatively extensive particular welfare of the individual and the family, the 'public' welfare lacks progress and stability" (III, 7). However, it can be said that ultimately the public welfare exists for the individuals.

It (the public welfare) finds its higher goal in the general welfare. On its part the public welfare merely offers the possibility for the general welfare, and this only insofar as the public means and conditions come into question. The general welfare as the private well-being of all the members is the immediate fruit of their own self-responsible activity which takes place, of course, by means of the guarantees and possibilities offered by the public welfare. For the public welfare the community is responsible; for the private welfare under

[18] For an excellent discussion of this point and the Peschian goal in general, see Jacques Yenni, "Pesch's Goal of the Economy," *Social Order*, I (April, 1951), pp. 169–76.

[19] Perhaps this offers a sound philosophic foundation for Wright's distinction between social security, the only kind of security he believes possible without cultural stagnation, and *personal* security, frequently confused by lay audiences with the former ("The Prospects for Capitalism," *Survey of Contemporary Economics, op. cit.*, p. 469).

normal conditions the citizen himself is immediately responsible (III, 747–48).

A difficulty may arise from the common Peschian expression, "the temporal goal of the individual is subordinate to the 'public' welfare as the goal of the political society" (I, 446). This may seem at first glance to be contradictory to the proposition that the public welfare has its higher goal in the general welfare of the individuals. But in the context of the subordination proposition "the individual" does not refer to all the individuals taken collectively, but rather to the individuals considered distributively. The restriction is that an individual must not interfere with or harm the public welfare, for the latter is a means common to all individuals whereby they are to realize their own welfare.

We now arrive at the central question: what is the material welfare of the nation, or national prosperity, or, in the term of Adam Smith, "the wealth of the nation"? The Peschian answer is:

> *To the prosperity of the nation appertains the permanent providing of the material means sufficient, in accord with the requirements of a progressive culture, for the satisfaction of the expanding wants of a nation increasing in population, so that along with a rather larger number of moderately wealthy persons, an extensive and capable middle class will be maintained, a living at least worthy of human dignity and corresponding to the degree of culture attained will be secured for all the members, even the lowest classes, permanent poverty remaining excluded—all of this, at the same time, with the protection of the higher values of the person, the family, the political society* (II, 316; italics in original).

It will be useful to examine this formula in some detail to clarify the sense of the expression, to explain its import, and to make evident many of the social criteria contained in it.

A "permanent" providing expresses the possibility of providing (*prosperitas publica*) as well as the actual provision (*prosperitas generalis* or *universalis*). That private enterprise is assumed is clear from the reference to a numerous moderately wealthy and extensive middle class; thus also self-responsibility is implied. A providing which is permanent or continuous requires an economy properly organized and guided by a sound economic policy in order to avoid or, at least, to dampen business fluctuations. Also implicit here is opposition to an unbalanced economy, one which is excessively dependent on factors beyond the control of the national economy. It should be noted that the positive expression of the importance of a social order offers a framework for an institutional approach rarely found in economic theory.

A nation increasing in population is assumed since the contrary is a manifest symptom of a sick and dying nation. The wants considered are all real, rational wants whose satisfaction depends on the possession of material goods. These wants are expected to be increasing both quantitatively and qualitatively in keeping with a progressive culture. For the economy is something living: "where there is life, there is development, progress" (II, 317). Moreover, all the people must share in this progressive culture, for culture is a common good.

That "a rather large number of moderately wealthy persons must be maintained" may be a surprising expression in the work of one who stresses the betterment of the conditions of the lower classes. But Pesch is a realist and is aware of the economic importance of this class. The hope to rise into the class of the wealthy is a stimulant to the independent middle class, just as much as the fear of falling into the class of the proletariat. Also, the rich have available means to follow intellectual and cultural pursuits which have an indirect economic effect. From the strict economic view, moderate wealth makes possible capital investment vital for a progressive economy.

An extensive middle class is considered essential to the harmony of society. In a society divided into only two classes, the rich and the poor, social unity is disrupted. Only where there is an even graduation from the lowest to the highest class, particularly with an extensive, economically independent middle class, is the absolute rule of a plutocracy excluded, and the proletariat lives not without hope. While the middle class may be measured by one's level of income, Pesch emphasizes the standard of one's economic and concomitant social position and function. Particular reference is to the small and medium independent farmer, the independent craftsman, businessman, and shopkeeper. Certain men can enjoy material goods and can feel prosperous only when at the same time they are independent in their work. In this economic autonomy alone can they find the possibility of the full and happy development of their capabilities. Even from the strict economic point of view, the small and medium-sized business, especially in the agricultural sphere, operates more economically than the large business. Also the craftsman can adapt his work more easily to the individual needs of the consumer and through the quality of his labor can maintain the quantity of his production even at the level of those who use synthetic productive devices.

The standard of living sought for the lowest classes in society, negatively, is opposed to the poverty and insecurity of the proletariat. In this sense it signifies an increased satisfaction of their needs. Positively, it is desired to lessen the gap between the standard of the wealthy and that of the poorest. Thus a more equitable—but not equal—distribution of income is a goal.

The higher values of the person, the family, and society must not be sacrificed in the striving for material goods, since an increase in the latter is not the highest measure of individual and social welfare. Material wealth is only one and not the sole element of social well-being.[20] For example, freedom is a part of the national welfare. Again, the worker often esteems the recognition of his equality as a man, the respect due to his person, the recognition of his importance for the common welfare as much or more than he esteems money and goods. Also, "if these pillars of the spiritual-moral order are overthrown, then material development is of no further use" (II, 333). As a general principle, the material welfare is subordinate to the spiritual-moral welfare. It must not be forgotten that "economic welfare also has moral and juridical foundations and limits, that on its side the earthly welfare constitutes the material foundation for all the higher striving of men and consequently may not come into opposition to the highest goals of life and to those moral norms which rule the whole of men's striving in their individual and social life" (II, 293).

Compare Pesch's concept of the national material welfare with the goals of the economy sought by Dr. Moulton: a progressively larger national income; a progressively wider division of income; a society in which individual rewards are based primarily on work performed; increasing economic security; the greatest possible development of the capacities of every individual; the opportunity for every capable individual to earn his own income.[21] In view of the close agreement of the two concepts it is significant that Moulton believes that the goals he presents in his book "represent the basic eco-

---

[20] Economists are becoming increasingly aware that economic or material welfare is only one element of total welfare; see Hazel Kyrk, "The Income Distribution as a Measure of Economic Welfare," *American Economic Review*, XL, Proceedings (May, 1950), p. 342; Harold F. Williamson, "An Appraisal of American Economic Progress," *American Economic Review*, XL, Proceedings (May, 1950), pp. 107–108, 117. It may be noted that Williamson (p. 117) expresses the belief that the goals of "a more equal division of income, economic security, and economic freedom" in many cases are "mutually inconsistent." They are not, however, *in se* mutually inconsistent, and one of the most important tasks of the organization of the economy, the concern of Chapter VII, is to investigate how the economy must be organized so that these heterogeneous goals may be harmonized.

[21] *Op. cit.*, pp. 142–48.

nomic objectives in which the American people are interested." [22]

But, after the determination of the content of the material welfare of a nation, a further question arises: what criteria are available to measure it? The problem, difficult in all cases, is rendered even more complex by Pesch's introduction of qualitative elements into the concept of material welfare. Since reference is immediately to a common condition in which all are to participate, before a nation can be called "prosperous" there must be evidence not only that the material means are being produced, but also signs of a possible or actual general sharing in the product. Furthermore, material welfare being only one important segment of total welfare, which also contains elements of the intellectual, moral, social and political orders, even the best information about the material side of life does not remove the impression of incompleteness.

> Many are rather skeptical about the whole theory of the criteria of national prosperity. Nor is this without reason, since thereby too often in a onesided manner that which is brilliant is stressed much more than that which is genuine in economic development; the dusty shadows which the extolled progress of production, of trade, inventions, machines, division of labor, etc., cast on the lives of men, are transformed into blazing light (II, 395).

The criteria offered by Pesch are meant to indicate only a conditionally true welfare—on the supposition that the supplying the members of the nation with material goods is not achieved through a sacrifice of the higher values of culture, morality, and religion.

Nor will any one particular criterion suffice as an indicator of the wealth of the nation; ". . . there is no single, inclusive yardstick that can be used" (II, 108). What is needed is a

[22] *Ibid.*, p. 148.

composite of various criteria; and even this is only a more or less limited representation of the material welfare of the nation.

The most reliable single criterion is per capita national income data (II, 110). This is particularly true if the income distribution pattern is included.[23] This may be very significant for "the diminishing of the economically independent middle class and the endangering of the secure basis of their income must be conceived as an unfavorable sign of economic development" (II, 380). Wealth statistics, though less significant than income figures, offer meaningful indications. For example, a concentration of property in the hands of a few is a sign of an unfavorable property and income pattern. The fundamental problem is that income and property are aggregate concepts, accounting concepts, while national prosperity is a concept of a condition or state.

The magnitude of foreign trade is frequently offered as a significant criterion. It is not rejected by Pesch, but its significance is qualified. A smooth, steady, equal rise in exports and imports is recognized as usually a favorable sign of an increasing economic development (II, 373). But if a shift occurs in the relation of imports to exports, then this change can be evaluated only by a study of the balance of payments. An "unfavorable" trade balance may be due to a genuine increase in domestic purchasing power, or may be artificially stimulated by domestic credit or foreign loans to the home country. On the whole Pesch favors domestic trade expansion rather than foreign, since its continuance is not dependent on conditions in the foreign country outside the control of the national economy. But, while not every increase of foreign trade is a favorable sign, "still let it not be disputed that the develop-

---

[23] Carl S. Shoup considers changes in *per capita* national income as "a partial indicator of changes in the material welfare of the group of persons making up the nation" ("Development and Use of National Income Data," *Survey of Contemporary Economics, op. cit.,* p. 311).

ment of foreign trade can be of the greatest importance for the prosperity of a nation" (II, 369).

A somewhat novel approach to evaluate the material welfare of a nation, suggested by Pesch, is to make a particular study of the welfare of the lowest classes. This is considered helpful, because it is an important fact in itself, and because if the lower classes are relatively well-off, it may be reasonably assumed that the higher strata of society are enjoying a correspondingly favorable position. The two major sources of measuring the well-being of the masses are real wage statistics and consumption figures. The former presents no difficulties, but the latter contains a series of steps. The final proposition is that the per capita statistics of the consumption of certain luxuries of the lower classes, such as sugar, tea, coffee, chocolate, throw light on the general conditions of the welfare of a nation. It is presumed that for the middle class, and *a fortiori* for the wealthy, the consumption of these comfort articles approximates the possible maximum. Thus an increase in the consumption of these goods within the nation as a whole indicates an increased consumption by the lower classes, and thus of their standard of living. Dwelling statistics also, particularly for the type of dwelling used by the lower-income groups, may be helpful here.

Although this Peschian concept of "national material welfare" does not permit the measurement of the wealth of a nation with any mathematical precision, it "suffices to call attention to some defects and to afford protection from an overevaluation of individual wealth phenomena in regard to its significance for the whole" (II, 334).

This general goal of the material welfare of the nation provides the framework for the determination of the more specific goals and criteria applicable to the various stages of the economic process. These more specific norms will be presented in subsequent chapters.

4. Social Philosophy and Ethics

Not specialization but isolation has been so prejudicial to the modern method of research. In this wise it could happen, for example, that economic theory became a materialistic and individualistic science of money-making, because its relation with the social sciences was completely forgotten. The wealth of the nation was unnaturally detached from the whole culture of the people, and thus the science soon became deprived of its subject matter (I, 498).

In these emphatic terms Pesch voices his contention that economics is an independent, but not an isolated science. To designate the autonomy of economic science and also the limitations of that autonomy, he makes use of the concept of a formal object, i.e., the particular aspect under which the various factors studied are considered. For the independence of a science is not sufficiently determined by pointing to a peculiar method of study. Autonomy rests on the fact that its subject matter is treated under an aspect different from the aspect under which any other science *ex officio* considers it. The formal object of economics is the providing for the material needs of the people, the temporal material welfare of the nation.

But an individual is unable to grasp fully the significance of a particular discipline if he does not know its relations with and its dependence on the other sciences concerned with the same subject matter. More specifically, Pesch contends that philosophic knowledge, both in the fields of social philosophy (as we have already seen) and epistemology, is necessary for the economist. "The economist must not only assemble, report, classify, and examine, he must also think and draw conclusions, proceeding from both a scientifically established philosophic knowledge and a correspondingly extensive positive erudition" (I, 565). For example, without a dependable philosophy the significance of the regularity observed in social phenomena, which is frequently called an "empirical law," can be misunderstood. It may be supposed that the social events in reality attributable to the motives of free men are rather to be subject to "causal laws" of the natural science type.

In the recent discussions the importance of social philosophy for economics has been affirmed by many authors. Fraser characterizes the "pure economist" as "the economist," who is more of an abstraction than "the economic man" ever was.[24] Even Professor Hicks admits that beneath Pigou's case of a divergence of the marginal social net product and the marginal private net product lies hidden "some of the gravest philosophic issues about the relationship between the individual and society." [25]

But whatever economists may hold in their methodological discussion, in practice the error has been not so much that philosophy has been avoided, but rather an insufficient philosophic position has been either explicitly or implicitly adopted. It is the opinion of Arther Salz that the inadequate philosophy of positivism has become "the official philosophy or the creed of economics." [26] And, according to J. M. Clark, the cultural lag found in the economic world, where the nineteenth century philosophy of individualism is now combined with group organizations possessing power for good or harm, is "one of the most threatening features of our whole situation." [27] A defender of utilitarianism, Frank D. Graham, holds: "Economics rests squarely on a cosmopolitan Utilitari-

[24] "How Do We Want Economists to Behave?" op. cit., p. 557.

[25] "The Foundations of Welfare Economics," Economic Journal, XLIX (December, 1939), p. 707.

[26] Op. cit., p. 17. Cf. Donald Wallace, "Monopolistic Competition and Public Policy," American Economic Review, XXVI (March, 1936), p. 85; also in Readings in the Social Control of Industry, p. 277.

[27] "Educational Functions of Economics After the War," American Economic Review, XXXIV, Proceedings (March, 1944), p. 64.

anism, and there is no way to get it off without a breach of all of the concepts that are the very essence of our discipline." [28] And Professor Parsons has pointed out that Lionel Robbins' criticism has merely demonstrated the weakness of associating economic theory with an inadequate utilitarianism, but not of associating it with *any* broader conceptional scheme. He concludes: "What is needed is not the repudiation of the relation of economics to social theory generally, but its integration with a better and more adequate social theory." [29]

Special consideration is also given by Heinrich Pesch to the question of the relation between economics and ethics or morals.[30] It is his firm conviction that economic theory cannot be dissociated from ethics or morals. Inasmuch as the theory of political economy is a practical science (which will be discussed below), it must remain in conformity with the moral law. Just as economics would hardly teach the physically impossible, so it should not represent the ethically reprehensible as a scientifically founded truth (I, 503).

His reasons for the necessary and useful harmony between economics and morals are: (1) The moral law has general validity for all times and places. It has reference to the free actions of men; and it is thus applicable to such actions in the field of economics. (2) The moral law directs men's actions to their last end; and therefore any contradiction of the moral law is a contradiction between the temporal and eternal end of man. (3) The economist cannot consider the formal object of his science except in relation with the general national wel-

---

[28] *Op. cit.*, p. 55.

[29] "Reply to Professor Knight," *Canadian Journal of Economics and Political Science*, VI (May, 1940), p. 469.

For a complete and competent treatise on the history of the relation of ethics to economics, see Joseph F. Flubacher, *The Concept of Ethics in the History of Economics* (New York: Vantage, 1950).

[30] Pesch makes a distinction between social philosophy and social ethics. The former determines speculatively the fundamentals of social life, e.g., the authority of the state or the goal of the economy; the latter is concerned with the moral goodness or evil of human acts.

fare. Thus he cannot forget the inner unity of the general culture and of the entire welfare goal of the political society. (4) The material welfare of a people is conditioned by the grade of morality existing in the economic life of the people. (5) The economist can receive from ethics aids for further progress in his theorizing (I, 504–507).

Nor were the many objections raised against this position ignored by Pesch. The two main ones will be discussed here. The first is that this would make economics a part of ethics; it would be a fusion of two disciplines which should be kept separate. He answers: no more than physics by accepting the laws of mathematics becomes a mathematical science. He insists on the proposition, already mentioned, that economics is an independent science, having its own formal object, which is different from the formal object of ethics, which is concerned with what is morally good or morally bad. Even the economic "should be" or "ought" is not an ethical proposal since directly it refers merely to what should be done in order that the goal of the economy be realized. The concern of the economist is "not to teach us about virtues and vices, but about the ways and means which lead to and preserve the material welfare of the people" (V, 93).

It should be noted that this difference of formal objects seems to have been overlooked by some economists who, appreciating the importance of ethics, wish to establish a phase or sub-division of economics to be called "the ethics of political economy" or "ethical economics." [31] This study, it is believed, combines the functions of the moralist and the economist, and can be completely dealt with either by the moralist with eco-

[31] Note the following statement of Professor Bye: "Ethical *economics* represents the overlapping zone between economics and ethics. It involves the application of standards of right and wrong to the institutions and processes which pure economics describes" ("The Scope and Definition of Economics," *op. cit.*, p. 636).

Cf. J. N. Keynes, *Scope and Method of Political Economy* (4th ed.; London: Macmillan, 1930), p. 61.

nomic training, or the economist trained in ethics. This is incorrect. If this study is to be made under the aspect of the morality of these economic actions, i.e., whether they are morally good or bad, then it is not an alternative proposition. An inquiry of this kind is the work solely of the moralist who has a knowledge of economics. The economist must be conscious of the morality of economic actions; but this neither requires nor permits him *qua* economist to *establish* the morality of such actions.

Pesch is insistent on the principle that to accept the findings of ethics, to respect the importance of morals in the field of economics does not require that the economist "becomes a moral theologian or a preacher of morals, or demand the good as good, or investigate or develop ethical principals and laws" (I, 531). In fact, he warns against an overemphasis of the ethical approach:

> Religion cannot produce grain; it cannot do away with physical evils. Morally advanced peoples will, no doubt, profit economically from the active, especially social, virtues of their citizens and will be better prepared to endure physical evil and hard times. But this does not mean that the economist should theologize or moralize in the treatment of his subject matter or, what is worse, try to derive an economic system from Holy Scripture. Medieval scholasticism, as well as present-day moral philosophy and moral theology, deals with the facts of economic life from a moral point of view. That is not the job of the economist. He will not, of course, oppose the demands of moral theology, but neither will he lose sight of the fact that economics has become an autonomous science, which treats of the economic life of nations from a viewpoint different from that of moral theology.[32]

---

[32] *Volkswirtschaftslehre der Gegenwart* I, *op. cit.*, pp. 202–3. Except for the last sentence, the translation is Franz Mueller's as found in his article, "I Knew Heinrich Pesch," *op. cit.*, p. 151. It is superior to the translation which appeared in my article, "The Welfare Economics of Heinrich Pesch," *Quarterly Journal of Economics,* LXIII (August, 1949), p. 356.

The second main objection is that economics prescinds in its theory from moral and ethical influences, while conceding them their place in practice. To answer this Pesch discusses the nature of abstraction. He recognizes the place of this methodological device in any scientific investigation, but is opposed to a wrong application of it. Abstraction should not degenerate into negation. The theorist in abstracting should not change the object being studied, and thus widen the gap between reality and theory. Nor is it enough to claim that non-economic motives are contained in the *ceteris paribus* of the demand-and-supply schedules, and then to carry out the analysis solely on the basis of self-interest.

The instinct of self-love as a strong motive in economic transactions is not slighted by Pesch. "The instinct of self-love will always be present, and in objectively morally indifferent matters will always obtain acceptance with most men" (I, 543).[33] But he disapproves of relegating moral considerations to the realm of scientific research of a troublesome incident. The mode and intensity of the economic motive changes not a little according to individual differences and circumstances, and is conditioned by the finer formation of a sense of honor and by the higher evaluation of ideals. "Actually," asks Pesch, "would not every economy and every state collapse, if the 'average' of its members were to permit themselves to be guided only by their own interest and would wish to deny every consideration except the 'principle of the smallest means'?" (I, 552).

However, Pesch would not deny that "pure theory," as a study limited to the natural instinct of self-interest, has significance for economic theory or possesses scientific worth. His objection is to calling such a study the complete science of economics. With Laveleye, he considers that it is merely the ABC of economic studies, which teaches "what *would*

---

[33] Cf. III, 6–9, where Pesch stresses the necessity of self-interest.

happen" if the economic development were permitted to run its full course under the sole and completely unrestrained operation of the self-love instinct. It is not a complete study of "what is" (I, 553). Self-interest is an instinct, an impulsive force and tendency within our human nature. Only it is not to be forgotten that instinctive forces are subject to man's reason: the guiding law of free rational men belongs to the intellectual and moral order. Personal utility is *a* motive, not *all* motives; and it is a motive, not a norm. To claim that an a-ethic theory is the sole valid economic theory would be a subjective "value judgment" of the highest doubtful value (I, 568).

5. A Practical and Normative Science

From the fact that the economy has a purpose, Pesch deduces the proposition that economics is a practical science. This is not synonymous with the statement that economics is concerned with reality, which all economists will admit. The question here is whether economic science is satisfied with truth for its own sake or whether it is seeking knowledge in order to achieve a goal. This does not mean that there is no place for pure speculation, but that the ultimate purpose of the science is to implement the goal of the economy.

A common source of confusion is avoided by Pesch when he distinguishes between the division into theoretical science and practical science and the terms theory and practice. Economics as a practical science is still theory. It includes theoretical elements derived from both speculation and observation; "but because it deals with the aim of the economy, it consequently reaches out to the organization of the economic process in relation to the social goal, and to this extent is a practical science" (I, 474, note).

Most modern economists, except the Robbinsian and the mathematical schools, consider economics a practical science. For example, to Hawtrey "it is beyond dispute that economic science is concerned with ends and means, and therefore with action"; [34] for Mitchell the importance of economics is derived "from the contribution it may make to welfare"; [35] in Wolfe's opinion, "Economics and political science are *purposive* sciences"; [36] Fraser believes that "in the social studies the end of knowledge is action." [37] On the other hand, Robbins, by rejecting consideration of the goal of the economy, by declining to permit normative elements in economic science, and by refusing to allow the economist *qua* economist to give prescriptions of policy, makes economic theory impractical for policy.[38]

Because this practical science is concerned with human conduct, Heinrich Pesch draws his final major conclusion: economics is not only a positive but also a normative science— a controversial proposition—maintained despite the intense criticism directed against it. Today it is probably the most disputed question in the matter of the scope of economics.

The German economist's argument for the normative character of economics rests on the nature of the object studied:

> If the economic process is not a matter of a "natural interrelationship," if it for the most part rests on the free actions of citizens, corporations, political judgments, on actions which in no way are "naturally" determined, which can be as they

[34] *Op. cit.*, p. 352.

[35] (Discussion) "Ethics in the Study of Democratic Politics," *American Economic Review*, XXXIV, Proceedings (March, 1944), p. 50.

[36] *Op. cit.*, p. 2. (Italics in original.)

[37] "How Do We Want Economists to Behave?" *op. cit.*, p. 570.

[38] For a confirmation of this judgment, note the criticism of Fraser: "They (Professor Robbins, Dr. Strigl, and their associates) hold economics to be scientific, not merely in the sense of pursuing objective truth, but in the narrower sense of seeking truth *for its own sake* (rather than for its practical usefulness) . . . (*Economic Thought and Language, op. cit.*, p. 30). (Italics and second parenthetical remark in original.)

are or could be otherwise, then it can hardly be understood how economic science, properly eliminates the question of an economic "should be," how it can renounce the prerogative of being a practical science oriented by a scientifically established and founded norm, and to this extent of being a normative science (I, 475).

In his discussion of the "new method" in economics, Pesch anticipated the objections of Robbins and his school—nor is this surprising for their doctrine is an anglicized version of the position of the German "pure" theorists, especially Max Weber and Richard Strigl. His criticism manifests a restraint and an appreciation of the commendable in their work.

> We proceed in this study in direct opposition to the new method in economics, which would exclude from economic theory every consideration of an end, every value judgment. If the advocates of this method would only say: "We will limit ourselves to the study of 'what is,' " there would be no reason to object to such a self-limitation. In fact there remains still much to do in economics in regard to the study of causal dependencies. But in most instances they go further: they wipe out from the field of science the problem of "what should be," with no consideration of ends, nor value judgments, since all this is unscientific. Moreover it leads to the question of a *"Weltanschauung."* But there no agreement prevails, and thus in economics, too, unanimity of opinion would be impossible. As if the followers of this method were united among themselves through the study of causes! That these economic writers uphold their position from wholly honest convictions should not be doubted. Too, the scientific productions of these eminent men stand in high esteem. Nevertheless the rejection of the consideration of ends by most of these scholars may be far more influenced by a distorted *"Weltanschauung"* than they perhaps believe.[39]

[39] *Ethik und Volkswirtschaft, op. cit.,* pp. 152–53.

Though some modern economists approve of the inclusion of both positive and normative propositions in economic science,[40] the more common position appears to be that of Robbins, who believes that there is a logical gulf between the two types of studies "which no ingenuity can disguise and no juxtaposition in space or time bridge over." [41]

Lionel Robbins would not completely reject normative statements, but they are to be relegated to the realm of "unscientific" welfare economics or economic policy. But, this would mean a conflict between theory and policy, a condition which Heinrich Pesch explicitly repudiates: "We cannot agree with the interpretation that wealth, welfare, productivity are the central notions of economic policy, while price is the central notion of economic theory" (I, 476, note 2). Economics as a science is distinct from policy, which is an art. However, art and science notionally include each other; for policy, if it is to be carried out completely and effectively, always presupposes a science. The fundamental norm for economic policy is the goal of the economy, which is the central notion of theory.

6. Conclusion

Heinrich Pesch explicitly offers an economic theory based on a definite social philosophy. Too often it is thought that

[40] See S. Moos, "Laissez-faire, Planning and Ethics," *Economic Journal*, LV (April, 1945), pp. 26–27; R. Hawtrey, *op. cit.*, pp. 362–65; L. Fraser, *Economic Thought and Language, op. cit.*, pp. 36–40, 50; R. Bye, "The Scope and Definition of Economics," *op. cit.*, p. 628; E. Walker, *op. cit.*, pp. 3–5, 210–27; Albert Wolfe (Discussion), "Undergraduate Teaching of Economics," *American Economic Review*, XXXVI, Proceedings (May, 1946), pp. 851–52.

[41] *The Nature and Significance of Economic Science, op. cit.*, p. 148. The treatment of the normative aspects of economics (pp. 147–51) indicates a lack of precision of thought. Throughout there is an unwarranted intermingling and synonymous use of the terms "normative" and "ethics"; indeed, Robbins seems to identify all normative studies with ethics.

the dichotomy is whether to accept a "neutral" economic science or one based on social philosophic principles. Actually, this is a false issue. At present there is no absolutely autonomous economic theory; and there is every reason to doubt that a theory of this type could be formulated and still be significant.

In the Peschian concept of the nature of economic science a methodological foundation is presented upon which to construct a theory of welfare, both scientific and significant. Perhaps it is what modern economists are seeking, a welfare economics in the tradition of Adam Smith, Marshall, and Pigou, but with individualism replaced by a sounder social philosophy more in keeping with the needs of our time.

CHAPTER THREE

THE THEORY OF CONSUMPTION

Because of his teleological approach, more than the usual lip-service is paid by Pesch to the importance of consumption in economic theory. This phase of economic life begins the treatise on the economic process. "The theoretical consideration of consumption must be the foundation and starting point of economic learning" (IV, 26). The aim of the economic process is to make possible a sound consumption in relation to the national welfare. And this possibility rests on the satisfactory provision of the people with attainable external goods sufficient to cover their needs. This must be the starting point of an economic theory which adopts the teleological approach.

The usual practice in conventional theory is either to relegate consumption to an appendix or to present some facts and figures on current consumption—a genuine theory of consumption is rarely found. The fundamental reason for this deficiency is that modern economics, fascinated by the determinate answers acquired by the natural sciences, spurns final causes, and devotes its attention to efficient causes or to the observation of mere functional relationships.

This exclusiveness even reaches the point where it demands the construction of a theory of "consumer-less economics." Economic phenomena are to be examined and explained in a spirit of complete detachment from the fact that the goods produced in the economy are destined—immediately or mediately—for consumption, that it is the consumer from whom proceeds the "demand" which, according to this very theory, is so important. Thus the economy is pictured as a round of acts of exchange wanting meaning and purpose, in itself a play of words, which has no intent to be of any value for anyone! Even the circles interested in social reform and economic policies succumbed too easily to the attractive problem of distribution and thus were unduly diverted from the investigation and clarification of consumption. In this wise consumption has not found the attention which it deserves.[1]

1. The Concept of Consumption

In general accord with economic tradition, consumption is defined as "the using up of goods for the immediate satisfaction of a human want" (IV, 25).[2] Reference is primarily to use-value, the destruction of exchange value being only a concomitant or consequent phenomenon. For in consumption we have the ultimate fulfillment of the purpose of the goods-world, when the use-value of goods accomplishes its function of satisfying wants.

The importance of a correct concept of consumption and the vexing problems involved in its formulation have been called to the attention of economists by the recent writings of Kenneth Boulding. He accepts the traditional formulation of

[1] Oswald v. Nell-Breuning, "Verbrauch," *Wörterbuch der Politik,* IV: *Zur Wirtschaftsordnung* (1949), col. 115.
[2] Cf. Marshall's description that consumption "is nothing more than a disarrangement of matter, which diminishes or destroys its utilities" (*Principles of Economics,* 8th ed., London: Macmillan, 1936, p. 64).

consumption as "the destruction of commodities—i.e., of valuable things—in the way in which they were intended to be destroyed."[3] The emphasis of his exposition brings out that

> It is not the *consumption* of goods but their *utilization* which for the most part gives us satisfaction. . . . For the great mass of goods . . . it is evident that consumption is merely a regrettable incident attendant upon their use, and if we had indestructible houses, furniture, clothing, china, etc., we would be much better off.[4]

Because of this, consumption in itself is not a reliable measure of economic welfare, and the Keynesian confusion of "consumer's expenditure" with consumption is misleading.

The contemporary Peschian, Oswald von Nell-Breuning, offers a variant formula which may aid in solving these problems. He distinguishes physical consumption, the actual using up of a good, from economic consumption—the concern of the economist—which is "the withdrawal of this good from the economic sphere, its dedication, surrender to an extra-economic purpose."[5] The effect in these two spheres may be simultaneous, as in the case of food; but frequently, as in the case of durable goods, the two kinds of consumption do not temporally coincide. One of the advantages of this formula is that it offers a simple solution for the vexing case, where the "consumer" is a collector acquiring goods not to consume them physically, but on the contrary to preserve them.[6] Also,

[3] Kenneth E. Boulding, "The Consumption Concept in Economic Theory," *American Economic Review*, XXXV, Proceedings (May, 1945), pp. 1–2. Cf. his *A Reconstruction of Economics* (New York: Wiley, 1950), pp. 135–37.

[4] Kenneth E. Boulding, "Professor Tarshis and the State of Economics," *American Economic Review*, XXXVIII (March, 1948), p. 101. (Italics in original.)

[5] Oswald v. Nell-Breuning, "Verbrauch," *op. cit.*, col. 116.

[6] The superiority of Nell-Breuning's concept of consumption appears in comparison with Marshall's treatment of the case of pictures, curtains, etc. The latter explains: "As the 'producer' of wheat is he who puts seed where nature will make it grow, so the 'consumer' of pictures, of curtains, and even of a house or yacht does little to wear them out himself; but he uses them

it avoids the confusion which has vexed the economist, when the "consumer" places back on the market the goods he has purchased, e.g., Wicksteed's house case.[7]

2. Consumer Behavior

Two diverse groups interested in different problems have aroused interest in the problem of how the consumer behaves. Robbins and Hicks through the debate on the problem of interpersonal comparison of satisfaction, and Keynes by introducing the propensity to consume as a factor in the savings-investment analysis and in the broader problem of full employment have raised significant questions about the consumer. Can and must we compare the satisfaction derived by different persons? How does the consumer think?

The objective level of satisfying wants in his analysis enables Pesch to avoid, for the most part, many of the problems involved in the interpersonal comparison of utility. On the subjective level he agrees with Robbins that one cannot measure exactly the satisfaction derived by the individual. "If an equal means of satisfaction quantitatively and qualitatively were divided among a number of individuals, through these same means equal satisfaction by no means would be obtained by the individuals, in fact for many there might be no real satisfaction at all" (I, 6).

On the other hand, on his normal level of analysis, with a value based on the objective circumstances, it is held that for the rich "100 marks have much less individual use-value than for the poor . . ." (V, 35). Use-value here is objective, in

---

while time wastes them" (*Principles of Economics, op. cit.,* p. 64). Time does consume them, but it is incidental to the main function of use. This approach gives the impression of resorting to a *refugium.*

[7] See Fraser, *Economic Thought and Language, op. cit.,* pp. 170–72, for a compact discussion of this case.

relation to the real wants of the individual, and is not directly concerned with the amount of satisfaction the individual may derive from the money.[8]

A related question, the answer to which is conditioned by one's position on the measurability of satisfactions, is how does the individual consumer think when he allocates his income. As Professor Haley has posed the question:

> Does he (the individual consumer) think in terms of the *relative* importance of a small increment in his rate of consumption of one commodity vs. that of another? Or does he think in terms of an estimated quantity of satisfaction to be expected from a small increment in his rate of consumption of a particular commodity? [9]

If the above question is taken as referring to objective satisfaction of wants and not mere subjective feeling, then it can be said that Pesch views the consumer as both comparing one commodity with another, and thinking in terms of the estimated satisfaction to be derived from a given commodity, in relation to the totality of wants which must be satisfied.

An example of the relative view is given, when it is claimed that if exchange value and price seem too high to the consumer, "many will forego the acquisition of the good, since with the same amount of money they can procure for themselves another useful thing which for them is more advantageous than the acquisition of the good in question" (V, 29–30).

But, for Pesch, this is merely a part of the process of the consumer's thought pattern. In the background is the totality of wants to be satisfied by the more useful goods. "In the

---

[8] On page 42, Volume V, Pesch uses the unhappy expression: "The giving up of 100 marks is felt very much differently by the poor than by the rich." But it is clear from his analysis that this "feeling" is based on objective individual circumstances.

[9] Bernard F. Haley, "Value and Distribution," *Survey of Contemporary Economics, op. cit.,* p. 6. The relative view is linked with the indifference approach; the small increment in the rate of consumption is the marginal approach.

market regularly the 'effective' demand does not include all persons and households for which a good in itself would be useful, but only those capable of paying and, *considering their totality of needs,* willing to pay for the goods" (V, 30).[10] Later Pesch explains that individual circumstances offer the solution to the question "whether one can pay such a price for such a good *in consideration of the total satisfaction of his wants,* which depends on the proper apportionment of income to the different particular wants" (V, 40).[11]

However, the Peschian analysis, as has been said, is primarily concerned with satisfying the needs of men. According to his terminology, "want" signifies from the personal side the lack of, the requiring, the necessity of the availability of an exterior means of satisfaction itself, according to kind, quantity, quality. Usually under need is understood the totality of wants, the means of satisfying these wants. Wants are a sign of the weakness of men, of their dependence, and also of their greatness, for as the culture of men develops their wants increase.

Besides the classification of wants into material and immaterial, innate and acquired, individual and collective, the most significant economic division is according to their urgency. These wants are sub-classified into existence or cultural wants (or necessities, comforts, and luxuries). With cultural progress the vital wants do not lose their force, but are now clothed in less crude forms. There is a greater choice of means to satisfy a particular need, so that a particular good now appears on a lower level of urgency.

Related to the classification of wants are the concepts, "standard of living" and "existence minimum." The latter refers to the minimum need of material goods which are physically necessary; but it is not synonymous with a "starvation minimum." Under the "standard of living" is understood

10 Italics in original.
11 Italics in original.

the degree of want satisfaction determined by custom and habit; it embraces existence, comfort, and luxury wants. It is not a physiological, but a cultural and social concept. Nor is it an immutable standard, but varies according to time, place, and station within society.[12]

In reference to wants, the problem again arises whether taken objectively they can be measured. Or, at least, can they be classified with any degree of scientific accuracy?

Pesch admits that "for the exact measurement of wants, taken in themselves and comparatively, a standard, a unit of measurement is lacking" (I, 8). Nevertheless, he believes that reason can construct on the basis of an estimate of their value a "stepladder" of wants according to their intensity and importance (see I, 7–8; and I, 27). In current terminology, Pesch denies a cardinal measurement of wants, and admits an ordinal measurement. This is important, for one of the functions of economic theory is "to recognize wants, to evaluate their urgency" (IV, 147).[13]

3. Consumption Criteria

One of the most significant features of Pesch's consumption theory is that the consumption pattern is not a datum. Various

[12] In a distinction foreshadowing Keynes' "propensity to consume" concept, Pesch divides income into "necessary" income which must be expended for the satisfaction of physical and social wants, and "free" income, that part which remains after the expenditures for one's living needs, and thus remains available to be freely expended by the consumer. The axiom is: "The smaller the income, so much the greater will be the part bound up with the necessary wants" (V, 551). Of course this is not original with Pesch, but is the so-called "Engel's law" publicized first in 1857.

[13] Cf. Raymond T. Bye, "Some Criteria of Social Economy," *op. cit.*, pp. 1–2. Bye recognizes the difficulties involved in classifying wants in the order of their importance scientifically in our present state of knowledge, and the problems arising in the application to concrete cases. Still he believes "that a systematic effort to catalogue a hierarchy of needs would not be altogether fruitless," and out of modern research, "it should be possible to set up reasonable requirements

criteria are offered with which to judge the suitableness of current consumption.

The fundamental criterion is that the more urgent needs are to be satisfied before the less urgent. It is required that

> first of all, the really necessary products be available in a supply sufficient for the people. After this the legitimate, progressive striving to provide useful and comfort things remains justified (IV, 315).

A related criterion is that a minimum standard is to be attained by all. The providing for the needs of the people in the sense of the material welfare requires that "an existence really worthy of a human being is secured and offered even for the lowest strata" of society (IV, 30; cf. II, 315). This does not mean, of course, that the level of consumption is to be equal for all.

Another criterion is that a fitting proportion must be maintained between present consumption and the provision for future needs, particularly through capital formation. In case of a conflict it is the present population which has prior claim to the goods of the economy. Nevertheless, "if the present does not understand how to limit its enjoyment, then it gives up the future to want and poverty" (IV, 131). The consumer must reflect how much of his income can be spent in a given time period without endangering the provision of his future needs. At the same time Pesch warns that not every form of saving is economically justified. He who economizes by the neglect of necessaries and suitable conveniences overstresses saving and converts it into greed.

Also, in the economy as a whole suitable provision must be made for the future by the maintenance and expansion of

---

for physical and mental health, and out of these it should be possible eventually to construct a general classification of wants in the order of their importance."

capital goods. But, at this level, too, the formation of capital at the expense of the satisfaction of the more important and more urgent present needs is not to be approved, for

> the formation of capital is still not an end in itself. Overcapitalization leads to crises in the sector where excessive expansion of production takes place (IV, 135).

The denial of the primary task of the economy, providing for the needs of the present generation, is never justified by pointing to the future possibility of increased production. "At the beginning of the machine age men offended against this principle; the formation of capital was overemphasized with the consequence that the laboring class suffered terrible conditions" (IV, 131–32). Pesch calls it an "erroneous" system, labeled "progress," which in order to accumulate capital to provide for future needs demanded an excessive curtailment of present consumption through the device of low wages. It is against the long-run interest of the entrepreneur himself to permit the health and strength of the laboring man to be impaired in this way.

> In brief, the consideration of future needs and, thus, the consideration of the formation of capital, is necessary and important. But still the increased and improved satisfaction of current consumption to a degree satisfying the demands of higher culture constitutes the first and most important sign of true progress. However the economy may be organized, never should the material means and power of production be increased by the injury of the personal factor (IV, 132).

Related to the criteria of a proportion between providing for the present and future needs is the question of over- and under-savings. Pesch considers it important that the consumer strike a balance between extravagance and excessive saving. Classical economics considered it always economically useful if the recipients of large incomes limited their consumption and invested the proceeds as new capital for productive purposes. Pesch believes this theory must be clarified and limited. Tacitly adopting the classical full-employment assumption, he holds it is correct not in regard to every luxury expenditure, but only in the case of the luxury

> which takes goods and labor power away from a better employment in the service of the national goal; which diverts industry, manufacturing and trade toward completely useless things; which because of uneconomic expenditures multiplies the number of the poor and embitters them; which harms, undermines, and damages the social and moral condition of the nation" (IV, 194).

Likewise must be qualified the Mercantilist argument (and perhaps that of some extreme Keynesians) which approves every luxury expenditure on the grounds that it increases the circulation of money. Unqualified this reasoning, to be logical, must finally come to the conclusion that the destruction of costly objects is to be welcomed as economically beneficial.

Finally, a relative optimum in consumption is reached only when the extrinsic standards of hygiene, esthetics, and morals are observed. Scientific health standards are important in the categories of food, clothing, and housing. At least the minimum requirements of calories specified by the medical profession should be obtainable by all; and the size of rooms and quality of homes should be in accord with modern hygienic studies. Esthetic standards are applicable in the matter of style of clothes, the ornamentation and decoration of buildings, the products of the glass, metal, and textile industries. The principles of morality offer the basis for a distinction between legitimate wants and cupidity. This safeguards economics from falling into materialism and cynicism. Also it serves as a guide to prevent resources from satisfying irrational perversions at the expense of the true and real wants of the people. Unless this distinction is observed, the incendiary must be called productive since, in the act of destroying, he at least has his own satisfaction (IV, 147).[14]

Is it possible, however, to establish objective criteria? In this matter no doubt the simplest case is that of hygiene. Medical studies can offer us objective requirements for the health of the nation, such as proper medical care, minimum standards of diet, etc. Also, the demands of morality, though without the same degree of unanimity, are embodied today in various local, state, and national laws. In general, it can be said that, while there are disputed marginal instances, there are also clear-cut cases about which communities can and do agree. In esthetics, boards of experts are able to agree on certain phases of their field—examples include city planning boards, music and art academies.[15]

It would be well to observe that a quasi-general agreement is desired not because this criterion decides whether a requirement is objectively legitimate, but because without such an agreement the practical application of a requirement may be unattainable. Also, while the emphasis in the establishment of standards is directed to the research and judgment of boards of experts, this in no way means that these boards are to impose their conclusions upon an unwilling consumer. Such studies are guides for consumers—as well as for economists and statesmen—who, within legal limits, may exercise freedom of choice.

4. Regulation of Consumption

These criteria offer a means of evaluating a given consumption pattern, or may be viewed as a model of what the optimum

14 There would be almost complete agreement between Pesch's position and the criteria offered by Raymond T. Bye in his excellent article, "Some Criteria of Social Economy," *ibid., passim.*

15 For examples of the appeal to scientific studies, see R. Bye, "Some Criteria of Social Economy," *ibid.,* p. 2; and E. Walker, *op. cit.,* pp. 255–58.

should be. To attain this optimum a certain regulation of consumption is required, which is to be performed by the consumer himself, the producer through vocational groups, and the state.[16]

The central figure to implement the consumption model is the consumer himself. In normal times the regulation of consumption is substantially a task "which the consumer guided by reason and conscience must accomplish for himself" (IV, 192). Pesch's teleological approach has particular significance in the question of "consumers' sovereignty." The importance of consumers' choice is emphatically recorded in the words of Schäffle,[17] approved and quoted by Pesch:

> In general, freedom of demand is certainly the most basic foundation of freedom. If somehow the means of life and culture were allotted from without according to each one's want pattern, still no one could live and develop according to his own personality; the material basis of freedom would be lost. . . . That one fundamental practical freedom—to use our private income according to our free choice—we would not be ready to sell for all the possible benefits of social reform lumped together (I, 388–89).

Also it introduces a new note in the discussion, for not only are the rights of the consumer stressed, but also his responsibilities. True progress in providing for needs is conditioned by the conduct of the consumer—how he is accustomed to satisfy his wants.

Besides the influence of the producer and the vocational groups on the consumption pattern, the state, particularly through its fiscal policy, can aid in attaining an optimum consumption. Because taxes and tariffs, especially on food and

---

[16] The role of the producer in this and wider contexts will be discussed in Chapter III; the role of the vocational groups will be found in Chapter VII.

[17] *Die Quintessenz des Sozialismus* (7th ed.; Gotha: F. A. Perthes, 1879), pp. 23–24.

clothes, influence consumption in varying degrees for the various income groups, a skillful selection and wise moderation in the inevitable taxes on consumption expenditures will make it possible to lighten in an essential way the burden weighing down the broad masses of the people (IV, 226). Furthermore, the state can exercise an indirect control over excessive luxuries by taxation laws, which should not, however, apply to works of quality or cultural accomplishments.

One of the most important tasks of the public authority in the field of consumption is to secure the guarantee of healthful conditions of living, where the proper care by the citizens themselves is not sufficient. The chief application of this is in reference to laws pertaining to food and medical supplies. But in regard to all goods the public authority should offer protection against falsification, adulteration of quality, where the buyer himself is not able to guard against such practices and where a sufficient control is not offered by private organizations, trade federations, and similar organizations. In principle, "products should be proved before they come into the hands of the ultimate consumer . . ." (IV, 234).

According to Pesch, luxury laws are not immoral, for the right to property is not absolute. But he believes such laws are impractical and carry with them the danger of unbearable bureaucratic intervention in the private life of the individual and the family.

CHAPTER FOUR

THE THEORY OF PRODUCTION

THE Peschian theory of production is concerned with the study of the concept of production and of the productive factors, and with the determination of criteria to be applied to this phase of economic life. This differs considerably from the modern treatment which, abandoning the traditional arrangement of the subject matter, considers the study of the factors of production more pertinent to the theory of distribution. "In the modern treatment," according to Professor Robbins, "discussion of 'production' is an integral part of the theory of equilibrium." [1] The normative aspects, of course, are considered foreign to scientific economic analysis.

The theory of production, for Pesch, is closely linked with that of consumption, the stimulant and regulator of production. Moreover, the pattern of consumer wants influences the whole form of the economy. For example, mass production is conditioned by a concentration of wants (IV, 804). Likewise

---

[1] *The Nature and Significance of Economic Science, op. cit.,* p. 71. See also his statement: ". . . in recent years economists have tended more and more to abandon the traditional arrangement. We no longer enquire concerning causes determining variations of production and distribution" (*ibid.,* p. 67).

the manner of production is not without its effect on the consumption pattern (IV, 169). Though the relation between the two spheres of economic activity is so close, Pesch believes there is a need of an autonomous theory of production which neither consumption theory nor price theory can satisfy.

"The securing of the supply of goods required for the providing for needs takes the first place" in the national economic approach (IV, 122). From the aspect of the individual consumer, it is his income in relation to the given prices which is central. But, in the national economic view, the first and most important step is a supply of goods. Next is the maintenance and development of the production process. Pesch is not very sympathetic with the social reformers who stress the need of a redistribution of income, but neglect the importance of production. "Production creates the goods by which men live" (IV, 123).

1. The Concept of Production

The central notion of production is an activity "which in the realm of the world of material goods creates or increases utility" (IV, 303). Or more technically, economic production is "that human activity or effect through which are acquired new substances (substantial change) for use in the providing for our needs with exterior goods, or whereby either a new accidental form or a new state is bestowed on an existing thing, matter, or being" (IV, 304).

To appreciate Pesch's analysis of the production process, it is necessary to understand the scholastic terminology employed, which is based on the Aristotelian taxonomy of causes. The pertinent forms are: (1) the efficient cause (*causa efficiens*) —that by which something is produced; this may be either a principal cause (*causa principalis*) or an instrumental cause (*causa instrumentalis*), the means or instrument which the principal cause uses to produce the effect; (2) the final cause (*causa finalis*) the goal of the producing activity; (3) the material cause (*causa materialis*) the matter out of which something is made; (4) the formal cause (*causa formalis*) which inheres in the matter and bestows on it either a definite being or an accidental appearance; (5) and, conditions which are not strictly speaking causes, but which positively or negatively influence the production—while they do not of themselves produce or enter into the productive activity, still they make the production possible or easy, by furthering the work of the productive causes or protecting them from disturbing influences (IV, 322).

According to this terminology, the principal efficient cause of production is, above all, human labor, both mental and physical. The final cause is the objective end which the work must fulfill, and the subjective motive of the producer. The material external world may enter into the production positively but passively, e.g., in the case of raw materials from which the finished product is made, or finished or unfinished material goods whose value is increased by transportation, storage, etc. The active part of the material external world is either as an instrumental cause, e.g., an axe, steam engine, coal, etc., which increases the productivity of human labor, or which more directly, as causes, cooperate with men to produce the product, e.g., steam power, electricity. The series of conditions furthering production are, for example, factory buildings, storage space, or in an exchange economy money to pay wages, buy tools and machines. The enterprise or the business organization itself is called a condition of production.[2]

---

[2] Some modern economists wish to call enterprise a fourth factor of production. Fraser has a useful observation on this trend and, also, the modern revised concept of capital, associated not with tools and machinery, but with the function of "waiting" or accumulating: " 'Enterprise,' the function of initiating

Conscious of the logical difficulties involved in the division of the factors of production in the traditional tripartite classes, Pesch nevertheless is willing to accept it if their relationship to each other is clearly understood. The difficulty is occasioned by the inclusion of capital as one of the factors of production. For Pesch capital is a cause or condition of production derived from the original factors, labor and nature, and subordinate to them in the production process. He thus sums up his position:

> We do not reject for the economic consideration a threefold division of the factors of production, but require that thereby each individual factor be assigned its correct place. The primary original factor of production is human labor-power and labor; the second is nature with everything in matter and power which is presented by it. Both together constitute the principal causes in production. What man creates through his labor by the utilization of the matter and power offered by nature does not constitute a principal cause, but is an instrumental cause or condition in the production process, consequently subordinate to the principal causes, particularly labor, the laboring men (IV, 327).

In the above discussion of the factors of production and the causes of production, reference was made to the final cause, subjective and objective. These concepts warrant a slightly fuller development, for they are important aspects for the determination of criteria for an optimum production.

---

production and/or of bearing the risks and uncertainties connected therewith, has acquired the status of a fourth factor, independent of the other three, at least in theory, and co-equal with them. And these corrections have altered the scope and meaning of the concept of a factor of production to an extent which has not always been fully realized. For neither 'waiting' nor 'uncertainty-bearing' are in any natural sense active participants in the productive process. They are important—and indeed indispensable—*conditions* of that process; for little if any production could take place without them. But they are not *parts* of it, nor elements in it" (*Economic Thought and Language, op. cit.*, p. 208). (Italics in original.)

From the private point of view the subjective motive (the *finis operantis*) is the profit motive of the individual producer. The objective purpose of the product (*finis operis*) is the use of the product, its capacity to satisfy a particular want of the prospective customer. On the national economic level, the objective goal (*finis operis*) of the whole economy is to satisfy the wants of all the people. At this national level, there is no subjective finis, for the national economy "lacks a subject, the subjective homogeneous bearer." [3] There must be a harmony of the various motives and tasks if production is to be called an optimum. In particular, there must be no disharmony between the producer's striving for a profit and the satisfying of the true needs of the consumer. "A production which seeks a private profit at the cost of the objective task, the providing for the need of the consumers, can under no aspect prevail as a well-regulated production, justified through the subjective purpose" (IV, 320).

2. Production Criteria

In the determination of the optimum production pattern the criteria developed in the theory of consumption are of the highest importance, for the highest norm also for production is the goal of the economy, the providing for the needs of all the people. This furnishes the frame of reference for the production criteria. And since the economy is concerned with scarce resources which must satisfy almost unlimited wants, the principle of opportunity cost is a serving principle which controls the discussion (see IV, 26).[4] In view of this goal and

[3] Heinrich Pesch, "Volkswirtschaftliche Aufgabe und Weltwirtschaft," *op. cit.*, p. 25.

[4] See note 13, page 85 of the subsequent Chapter V, for the place of "opportunity cost" in Pesch as a tool of a national economic analysis, but not on the level of private enterprise.

this condition the welfare of the people demands of production that: (1) the really necessary products be produced first, then the useful, and finally the convenient; (2) what is produced must not harm the material and spiritual health of the consumer; (3) the manner of producing must not endanger the higher social values (IV, 315).

The first criterion is a recognition of the sovereignty of the goal of the economy and the significance of the principle of opportunity cost. An expanding production output is presupposed, since the economic task is viewed as a progressive goal, requiring an increased supply of goods, "even apart from an increase in population" (IV, 328). However an increased supply of goods in itself does not signify economic progress. The latter depends on this: "that production advances in those spheres in which the satisfaction of the most important and most necessary needs of men depend; that the people have at their disposal better food, better clothes, better dwelling places" (IV, 121). This requirement is not satisfied if economic resources are concentrated in an unequal fashion, so that the providing for other, perhaps more urgent, needs has to be curtailed. The second and third criteria could be grouped together under the rule of the extra-economic criteria of ethics and hygiene.

Moreover, a certain dynamic aspect is introduced in that wants are not considered static and given. "Wants are not always the same; they change with time and with men according to kind, standard, and number" (IV, 318). This requires a balance between production and consumption. Normally, an increased production presupposes an increase in consumption. If production increases too rapidly in proportion to consumption, it is just as harmful to the economic system "as an excess of food for the body" (*ibid.*). Included in this requirement is that not only the wants but also the buying power of consumers must be in harmony with production.

"A disproportion between production and consumption arises particularly because the buying power of the masses, as a consequence of a defective economic organization and income distribution, do not increase in the same measure as would correspond to the given productivity of labor" (IV, 318–19). Thus either over-production or under-consumption would offend against this precept.

On the level of the firm, the task to satisfy the needs of his prospective customers demands of the producer: (1) a correct choice among the different possible applications of matter and power; (2) a consideration of actual given conditions of the prospective customers; (3) the application of the principle of economy.

In the reference to the first principle technology limits the possibilities of a choice of the combinations applicable to the production of the physical product. And, "within these limits the economic factor chooses and decides such tasks for the technology which correspond in the best possible way to the economic goal of providing for the designated needs" (IV, 307).

Pesch recognizes that it is not always easy to fulfill the second principle, for in the modern economy, particularly in regard to export products, the wants of the consumers for a particular product are difficult to estimate. But, every endeavor must be made to do so, for the fulfillment of the economic goal of the economy depends thereon. "It cannot be sufficient to produce products which are not desired as goods" (*ibid.*).

Finally, the third firm criterion requires that for the production of the individual product, more goods and power must not be employed than the attainment of the *finis* of the particular production demands.

> Every useful thing should be striven for and attained with the least possible cost. The production must also in this sense be "economic" (*ibid.*).

Besides these general principles, a series of more particular requirements is listed, which the consumer may and can demand of the producer. These include: (1) excellence in production, with particular reference to the standards of hygiene and the quality of the work performed; (2) fairness, honesty, and truthfulness in the execution of the production and the offering of the product—special attention is given here to advertising; [5] (3) a just price; (4) and, in order that these pertinent requirements may be fulfilled, progress in business education, a development of the individual producer's business knowledge,[6] and an intensification of his moral education.

It is noteworthy that in this entire discussion of production criteria, no mention has been made of the laws of increasing and diminishing returns.[7] Though not mentioned in this context, these laws are not ignored by Pesch, but are applied to another, wider problem, the relative fruitfulness of industry and agriculture.

Interested in the fostering of the agricultural sector of the economy, Pesch is concerned to refute the position—put forth by some economists—that industry is subject to the law of increasing returns, while agriculture is governed by the law of decreasing returns. But the law of decreasing returns is in itself not a social law, but a law of nature, a natural-technological phenomenon. And, points out Pesch, the supposit, even expressed explicitly by many economists (e.g., Senior, Mill, and Marshall), is that the art of agriculture remains the same. He observes that

[5] Pesch is not opposed to advertising *in se,* but merely to the abuses of advertising. See IV, 174–77.

[6] The scope of the knowledge required of the producer extends from general business to psychology. See IV, 183–86.

[7] One reason for this hiatus may be that these laws are based on a marginal analysis which Pesch accepts only with qualifications. See IV, 310–11, note 3, where Pesch expresses his doubts about the wisdom of the extensive application of the "law of diminishing returns" to all the production factors, as the American economists have done.

all moderate defenders of the law of agriculture hold this merely as a conditional, temporary law with the state of entrepreneurial skill remaining the same. If this state of enterprise skill changes, if "the arts of agriculture" improve through progressive agriculture technique, increased employment of suitable machinery, suitable business organization, the acquirement of by-products, etc., thus an increase of yield is indeed possible, without increasing—perhaps at first, with a lowering of—the per unit cost of production (IV, 853).

Furthermore, Pesch rejects the position that industry is characterized by the law of increasing returns. Also in industry at some point the realization of increasing returns gives way to the law of diminishing returns. The various reasons why industry cannot continually expand with increasing or constant returns are: (1) The individual business becomes too complicated; (2) a limit is reached in the effective, intensive division of labor; (3) the number of favorable industrial locations, e.g., water-power sites, are limited; (4) the required continuous and increasing market for the product, on the national and particularly international level, becomes more uncertain (IV, 856–61).[8]

Pesch's position is not that agriculture should be advanced at the expense of industry; but that industry should not be advanced at the expense of agriculture. He seeks a balanced economy, as far as this is practical.

In conclusion, it may be mentioned that the goal of the economy, set forth as the regulating principle of production, is considered too as the measure and the limit of economic freedom in production. This guiding norm

---

[8] Julius Wolf's "law of declining capacity for progress" which Pesch alleges against the possibility of increasing returns in industry does not seem valid (IV, 857). Absolute figures are offered (e.g., thread has declined from 38 shillings a pd. to 1 schilling and 10 pence) to show that the same gain cannot be expected in the future. But, obviously, the same *rate* of decline has not been excluded.

requires this freedom where and to the extent that it leads to a more abundant provision for the people, but demands the limitation of freedom where it stands in the way of this provision. Therefore it does not exclude competition insofar as competition can lead to the expansion of production, to the increase and improvement of the product, to the more accurate adaptability to needs, to a technical and economic perfecting of the production process and to the greatest possible reduction of the cost of the product (IV, 321).

CHAPTER FIVE

A TELEOLOGICAL VALUE AND PRICE THEORY

Perhaps nowhere is the similarity so close and the difference so fundamental between Heinrich Pesch and the modern theorist as in the treatment of value and price. The competitive price is designated as the optimum, because it is the closest expression of the objective value of goods. But a paradox emerges, for while the competitive price is the optimum, it is claimed—contrary to the assumption of pure theory—that free competition leads to a divergence from this optimum. Competition tends to its own self-destruction. Moreover, "Big Business," monopoly, cartels (oligopoly), and bilateral monopoly are not considered as extraneous adjuncts to price theory, but are recognized as prominent market forms. In both conventional and Peschian policy a price equal to the competitive is sought. The "pure" theorist hopes to attain this goal through the restoration of competition; Pesch looks to the establishment of order in the market.

Consistent with his general approach, Pesch makes the idea of the goal of the economy the central core of his value theory.

70

He thus characterizes his own form of utility value theory as a "teleological system of value," in contrast to cost of production theories, the "causal systems" (I, 52). The decisive factor is "not what goods are because of men, but what they signify for men" (*ibid.*). Ultimately the point of view of the consumer, not of the producer, is the important one. This teleological theory is both subjective and objective, and combines both absolute and relative features.[1] It explains the value of an economic good by its socially evaluated utility and scarcity.

Before explaining in detail Pesch's theory of value and price, a word may be in order regarding the importance of value theory, since modern theory is chiefly concerned with market value—even exchange value in the sense of a normal being pushed into the background or eliminated entirely. But can price or market value alone suffice to answer all the important questions of economic life? In a "value-free" social economics, such as Cassel's, in which price is based merely on the cost principle, certain general judgments of men are ignored. For example, unanswered are such simple questions as the buyer's, "Is this product worth as much as its price? Is this price too high or too low?" Unanswered, also, is the producer's, "Will there be enough prospective buyers to whom this product will be worth more than the cost?" (see V, 83).

Moreover, on the higher level of the national economy concerned with national income and wealth, "goods on the whole are of importance not because of their exchange value, but because of their 'being,' their usefulness as means of enjoyment, precisely for the satisfaction of wants, the acquiring of comfort and all those things pertaining to the well-being of a nation" (II, 115). Unless market valuations are to be accepted

---

[1] Pesch explicitly rejects, as leading to error, the division of value theories into the classifications "objective" or "subjective" theories, particularly regards utility and cost theories. He recommends in their place the terms "teleological" and "causal" (I, 53). Despite this, Harris continually refers to Pesch's value theory as an "objective" theory (*op. cit.*, pp. 43–45).

as a datum, so sacred that no investigation of the merits of the evaluation are to be made, a theory of value is required which will go behind the conventional supply and demand curves, or the indifference curves. Also, a value theory bears important policy implications. Historically both cost and marginal utility value theories have been used to cast light on the important questions of competition and the equality of incomes.[2]

1. Economic Value and the Community Evaluation

The establishment of the optimum price pattern is considered of importance by Pesch. For, the price is viewed as furnishing the basis of all economizing. It is the regulator of production, since it "stimulates the discovery of the lowest cost value and the search for the highest use value" (V, 35). For the consumer "the price of the individual good determines the measure of consumption, rules the choice of the means of satisfaction with a given income" (V, 36).

It would be difficult to find a more generally accepted proposition in economic theory than that the competitive price is the optimum price. This classical heritage has recently been forged by Lange *et alii* into an essential tool of the economic theory of socialism. And, also in the Peschian price theory this dictum has found a central place. For example, in the treatise on value it is stated that demand and supply "by their competition are able to bring about such a determination of value, which most corresponds to the fundamentals of objective determination" (I, 49).[3] More specifically, in the treatise on price

---

[2] See Lindley Fraser, *Economic Thought and Language, op. cit.,* pp. 114–15. Also Stephen Enke observes: "One of the main potential uses of value theory to the economist is as a predictive aid. This is particularly so, when as is often the case, the economist is concerned with public policy" ("On Maximizing Profits: A Distinction between Chamberlin and Robinson," *American Economic Review,* XLI [September, 1951], pp. 566–67).

[3] By a careless translation of the German "am meisten" which he makes

it is claimed "on the supposition of normal conditions, this whole process of trial-and-error in the determination of market price will lead to the approximately correct result; the market price can be considered as the approximate value with reference to the objective factors ultimately determining the exchange value . . ." (V, 37). And with normal conditions the market price is called "the socially normal price" (V, 52). Finally, the competitive price is shown to equal the just price, for the same factors are the determinants of each, so that to the competitive price is credited the "presumption of justice" (V, 93).

What is meant by competitive price? Rigid economic theorists describe the competition necessary to achieve the optimum price as taking place in a market in which there are numerous and small sellers compared to the market, in which there is a homogeneous product, perfect mobility of resources, and perfect knowledge and foresight on the part of each participant. Because of the impossibility of realizing such ideal conditions, and also because of the intrinsic inconsistencies involved, more moderate theorists speak of a "workable competition," whereby the unrealistic assumptions of perfect knowledge and mobility are modified, place is provided for differentiated products, and the emphasis is on the ease of entry into an industry or market.[4] It is with this "workable" species that Pesch's description of competition conforms. It posits as necessary assumptions: (1) goods that reach the con-

---

read "at most" instead of "most," Harris gives an incorrect impression of the force of this sentence (*op. cit.*, p. 42). There is a great deal of difference in emphasis between the two words. "At most" is simply a mistranslation of the German superlative.

[4] Cf. J. M. Clark, "Toward a Concept of Workable Competition," *American Economic Review*, XXX (June, 1940), pp. 241–56; also in *Readings in the Social Control of Industry*, pp. 452–75; *idem, Alternative to Serfdom* (New York: Knopf, 1948), pp. 61–83; Howard S. Ellis, "Economic Expansion Through Competitive Markets" in *Financing American Prosperity*, Paul T. Homan and Fritz Machlup (eds.) (New York: Twentieth Century Fund, 1945), p. 177.

sumer via a market exchange; (2) goods of general use; (3) a true supply and demand; (4) a suitably large, regular, well-organized market (V, 36).

But more interesting and more fruitful is an analysis of the concept of the optimum. In what sense is the competitive price the best, and why? It is a commonplace in economic theory of all brands that the competitive price is the most desirable, for it equates marginal cost with price (marginal revenue) and thus assures the maximum aggregate production and the best possible allocation of resources. The question is left open, however, as to *why* the marginal evaluation in the market is accepted as relevant. By implication this may mean: (1) the average individual judgment is accepted as the best; or, (2) it is not known what is best, so the prevailing social philosophy is accepted which holds that consumer preference as expressed in the market is best.

The Peschian explanation why competitive price is the optimum is that it equates average competitive cost with social use-value, which is equivalent to saying that marginal cost excluding rent equals marginal revenue, for in competition the supply curve is the average cost function including rent and also the marginal cost function excluding rent, and the demand curve is the marginal utility.[5] The particular contribution to theory is found in Pesch's explanation of why this is significant and how it is attained. His analysis is more fundamental than that offered by current theory. It is claimed that ultimately the competitive price is the optimum because it provides best for the needs of the people. And it achieves this goal of the economy by determining the real economic value via the "communis aestimatio" which expresses the real

[5] This proposition follows from these two basic propositions: (1) the demand function is average as a revenue concept, and is marginal as a utility concept (the latter is the significant concept for welfare economics); and, (2) the average cost including rent equals marginal cost excluding rent (welfare economics seeks to equate the latter with marginal utility).

exchange value. But to appreciate this position it is necessary
to understand the Peschian concepts of economic value, exchange value, and the "communis aestimatio."

Economic value, taken formally as a universal concept, is
defined: "The estimableness of economic goods because of
their usefulness and their necessity for the satisfaction of
human wants, or on account of their importance for the
material welfare of men" (I, 25). If the consideration of economic goods is in reference to general human wants, then
their value refers to an *abstract, generic* class value. On the
other hand, if the special wants or desires of an individual,
or the particular advantage accruing to him from a definite
good because of his personal, individual circumstances or his
personal preference, are considered, then it is a question of
the *concrete, individual* value of this good for the particular
person.

This individual value, according to Pesch, may be called
subjective, in the sense that it looks to the importance of a
good for the interest, the welfare of a definite person. It answers the question: what is this thing worth to me? Objective
value is the importance of a good for the attainment of an
end, the realization of a goal in itself. It answers the more
general question: what is this thing worth? "A quantity of
food has this or that objective food-value, a cord of wood this
objective heat-value for the poor as for the rich; the subjective
value, however, varies according to the special circumstances
of the different subjects" (I, 26; I, 53). Apparently, the reason
why Pesch uses the terms objective and subjective in this context is that the general value is the pure expression of the
objective factors determining value, while the individual re-
flects these objective properties colored by the subjective
circumstances. But it would seem better to use the terms general (or social) and individual. For, there is a more universal
sense in which the terms objective and subjective apply to

value, not only to both general and individual economic value, but to every species of value, whether esthetical, moral, etc.

Objectivity pertains to all forms of value, since the *basis* of an actual evaluation is a property of the thing to be valued. Actual evaluation is a judgment of recognition which does not create value but rather presupposes it. A thing is estimable before the human mind makes its judgment and it remains such even if no one thinks of it. The nature of this objectivity, however, must be clearly understood.

> If value, estimability, is called an objective property of a good, still it should not therefore be said that it is in itself an absolute property pertaining to the physical being of the thing, in the same sense as weight, light, etc. The concept of value comprehends the objective perfection of a thing rather in its relation to an ideal, an end, a goal, a want, etc., and to the possible evaluation in respect to this relation. The work of art is estimable, since and insofar as it corresponds to a cultural ideal—a souvenir of a deceased parent on account of its connection with the departed one, food on account of its usefulness for the purpose of nourishing, etc. (I, 20).

This stress on the objectivity of value in no way is to be taken as a denial of the subjective factors involved. As Pesch says, "It hardly needs to be mentioned that subjective forces exercise a more or less great influence on the judgment of value" (*ibid.*). Subjective coloring is given to the judgment of value, since individual ideals, outlook, wants, and want experiences are not the same for all individuals. But such purely subjective motives in the act of judging no more destroy the objectivity of value than they destroy its objective basis in the thing evaluated. Consequently, in spite of many differences a significant agreement in judgments of value always remains within the realm of possibility. In fact, it is in this general judgment that the "objective" value finds its expression (I, 21).

This objectivity of value should not be considered something immutable. There is a certain "relativity" in the formation of value.[6] Changes in a cultural milieu can produce changes in the objective value of a thing. For example, variations in the want pattern of a group for a particular product or for other products may bring about changes in the economic value of this particular product. And an important influence in the formation of a want pattern is the relative size of the income, especially of the masses. Because of the influence of nature, fixed customs, and durable acquisitions, demand is the more stable, slow-changing phenomenon in the historical development of a nation. Also, variations in the economic value of a product may be influenced by changes in the supply of this product or other products. Long-run mutations in the supply are due to variations in the process of production: changes in the productive power of land, nature in general, and the labor force, in the produced means of production, the level of technology, or the existing forms of social and business organizations. Of these forces influencing supply, nature and land are relatively fixed, the remainder more elastic (see I, 28; V, 48).

In the last analysis the measurement of the value of a definite good or class of goods depends:

> (a) on the nature and the intensity of the wants which can be satisfied by the good. Just as men's wants are not all of the same type, but are of different importance and intensity, likewise there corresponds to this order of wants on the side of the material goods an order of value;
>
> (b) on the specific and individual properties of the eco-

---

[6] Value is relative in other senses besides that of "mutability" given in the text. Every value is essentially a relation of an objective property of a thing to an ideal or an end. Consequently, in economic value there is the relation of utility, as a means, to human welfare, as an end. And exchange value is a question of the relation of comparison of one economic value with another (see I, 53).

nomic good with reference to the satisfaction of human wants;

(c) on the scarcity of the goods, i.e., on the proportion between the stock and need, and in conjunction with this, on the difficulty, effort, labor, material outlay, the cost required for the production of a definite type of goods;

(d) on the particular wants, circumstances, the economic condition of those persons making the evaluation (I, 26).

The most fundamental objective reason and basis of this value determination—and not a mere supposit—is the usefulness of the economic good to satisfy human wants. What is absolutely useless has no economic value; and what is useful, but present in unlimited supply (free goods) likewise lacks economic value. Thus, the degree of the value of economic goods rests not only on the qualitative factor but also on the quantitative (I, 26–27).

With Adam Smith, Pesch distinguishes two fundamental senses of the concept economic value: "use value" and "exchange value." [7] These two senses, however, are not two coordinate species of value, to be placed on the same line; rather, exchange value is subordinate to use value. There is really one value divided according to two different states of employment, use and exchange.[8] In view of the goal of the economy, use value is the all important type, for it answers the question: what is this good in itself worth for men? Subordinate to this, although of high practical importance, is exchange value, which answers the question: what is this good worth in comparison with other goods? Use value represents the economic

---

[7] Pesch criticizes Smith for an improper definition of use value and for neglecting the concept in his further treatment of value.

[8] Fraser, who distinguishes four senses of the word value, states: "Note that they do not represent four *kinds* of value. We have no ground for supposing that they are coordinate species of a genus and that there is a fundamental concept of 'value as such' of which they are the forms or expressions" (*Economic Thought and Language, op. cit.,* pp. 59–60). Pesch seems, however, to disagree on the latter point that there is not a fundamental concept of "value as such."

value of goods in respect to the satisfaction of human wants; exchange value represents the same value in regard to its migrations in exchange (I, 41–42).

This brings us to the second essential concept in the Peschian theory of value, the analysis and exposition of exchange value. Here it is a question only of the *social* exchange value, abstracting from the particulars of individual exchange. Exchange value appears as a quantitative relation, the proportion wherein the use value of one type is exchanged for the use value of another type. To express fully the fundamental of exchange value, Pesch defines it: "The exchange value of a good or quantity of goods is the economic value of the same in its capability of being substituted by the economic value of another good or quantity of goods, determined and measured by the general evaluation" (I, 47). Or briefly, "Exchange value consists in the quantity of goods, which the good in normal circumstances will obtain" (*ibid.*).

The theoretical problem in exchange value is the search for the common denominator which gives unity to the exchange. For, as objects of use, goods are materially different things. In the Marxian system this unity is said to come from the common denominator, socially necessary labor or labor-time. But, as Pesch argues, goods are exchanged; and they are constituted goods, only causally, not formally, by labor. Their properties are the important factor. Men do not strive for goods because of the labor time contained in them but because of their ability to satisfy human wants. And it is from this common property, use value, whence comes the unity necessary in exchange (I, 43–44).

A distinctive feature of Pesch's value and price theory is that price is not conceived as always equal to exchange value—a divergence of price from the socially normal exchange value is considered possible. This is, of course, in contrast with the conventional position that price and exchange value are always equal. The immediate explanation of this difference in opinion is that Pesch is considering only the socially normal exchange value, which he holds as the sole significant exchange value, while the conventional theorist limits himself to an individual *ad hoc* exchange value.

But, behind this surface difference lies a more fundamental disagreement concerning the nature of exchange and the ruling principle governing it. In the Peschian system exchange is *motivated* by the difference of the individual use values of the articles to be exchanged—(comparison of the individual use values). It is ruled, however, by the principle of the equivalence of exchange value—(comparison of exchange values). This equality of exchange value pertains to the essence of exchange, for it *is* an exchange, not a gift. To Pesch it is a special case, an exception falling outside normal exchange relations, when a person's desire, because of an exaggerated personal inclination or an intense personal need, is so great that he will or must buy no matter what he must exchange for this desired object (V, 19).

Opposed to this principle of equivalence is the opinion that the governing principle of exchange is the mere "consent," the mere free agreement, the mere free will of the contracting parties. Implicitly, at least, the conventional acceptance of price as always equal to exchange value is based on such a "consensus" theory. To Pesch this view exhibits a two-fold error: (1) it assigns to the will of the contracting parties something that pertains to their judgment; (2) it attributes to the contracting parties a type of will which they do not possess.

For, basically, men cannot be arbitrary in the evaluation of things. "Can a man judge a flask of air to be of the same value as a flask of wine?" (V, 19)

> Why is such a judgment impossible? Since the air is available to everyone; the wine, on the contrary, is scarce, much labor

being required for its production and much care for its preservation. The estimation of value is precisely a judgment of reason, recognizing the objective factors, which exist independent of the free will of men. . . . If, too, either by deception or force, by being misled or being intimidated, the freedom of one of the parties is either entirely destroyed or at least diminished, if need compels him to trade with a loss, if more is snatched from him than he intends to give up, this violation of equivalence is as much dishonest gain for the other party as is the purse which the traveler "freely" gives to the robber in order to save his life (V, 19–20).

Ultimately, this question is the even more basic one concerning the objectivity of economic reality. Pesch's position is opposed to the subjective approach with its acceptance of only the data of the market-place as the sole concern of the economist. In the Peschian system equivalence of exchange value has real, objective, though mutable, factors behind it.

Exchange is not limited to profiteers and idiots, who agree upon "real" prices without any consideration of the exchange value. It takes place, as we presume, regularly between honest and rational men (*ibid.*).

Or, to put the objectivity problem in terms of supply and demand analysis this means that "supply" and "demand" do not always represent the objective factors "stock" and "need." If supply and demand always actually and certainly represented stock and need, for Pesch "there would be no reservation to be made regarding the determination of price by supply and demand" (V, 28). For in this case the "price is determined according to the exchange value," which is in turn determined by the objective factors (*ibid.*). But, actually supply and demand as the free actions of interested persons do not always truly represent real demand and, especially, the real supply.

Products can be held back, a feigned need can cause an unreal demand—both for the sake of gain. Free competition can offer no satisfactory guarantee against these (V, 29).

This consideration of the rational nature of exchange will later have important significance for policy. For, if every price that is agreed upon is not necessarily to be accepted as in keeping with the true exchange value, and if exchange value is considered the reflection of the true use value of the goods, then there is room for questioning certain segments of the price pattern.[9]

How is this normal social exchange value determined? To explain the process of exchange value determination Pesch introduces the third essential concept of his value theory, the *communis aestimatio*—the social, i.e., general evaluation within society. But, then how is this general evaluation formed?[10] Obviously, goods are not exchanged by themselves; they are exchanged by men. Nor do these goods have their exchange value stamped on them by nature. The formation of exchange value is the work of the human mind, compre-

[9] "'If one does not hold the conceptual distinction between exchange value and price which is a consequence in exchange of exchange value,'" says Schäffle (*Gesellschaftliches System der menschlichen Wirtschaft* I[3], 1873, 218), "'then unexplained is the constitution of a socially, economically normal value, the arising of prices from the quantitative conjuncture of many degrees of cost and use value united in supply and demand, and the standard reaction of the price on these proportions'" (V, 26, note).

[10] Harris has charged: "But how social esteem determines exchange value, conceptually or concretely, or how, indeed, the *aestimatio communis* is itself determined, is never really explained. He (Pesch) only tells us:

With respect to goods, for which there exist normal exchange relations in a wide circle of persons, there thus develops by virtue of experience within this circle a value-judgment which brings to expression the actually recognized and, accordingly, generally valid value for these persons and economies. This general validity is demonstrated in its normal application in exchange (V, 16)" (*op. cit.*, p. 44. (Parentheses added.)

Apparently Mr. Harris overlooked Pesch's general treatment of this problem in Volume I, pp. 44–46; and the specific exposition in Volume V, pp. 36–38 under the very title "General Evaluation and Market Price"; and pp. 40–41 under the title "Individual Evaluation and Market Price."

hending, judging, and actually evaluating. Thus, exchange value appears formally only in the human mind; outside the mind there is only the good with its perfections, properties, and definite quantity relations (I, 47).

This evaluation is not something arbitrary, but normally will have as its foundation the objective factors on which its grade of exchange value rests. These objective factors are to be sought first of all in the general economic value, and secondly in the particular circumstances of society. As mentioned above, the economic value depends on the qualities of the good which enable it to serve as means for the satisfaction of human wants, and on the scarcity of the good. The special circumstances of society are part of the objective foundation determining the general evaluation to the extent that, in addition to the natural wants, consideration is taken of the habitual wants determined by custom, and that the supply is conditioned by the particular marketing practices of the community.

How, then, does the *communis aestimatio* take into consideration these objective factors? Is it true, as has been charged, that the *communis aestimatio* is "independent of individual evaluations" and that "Pesch's thinking is controlled by the notion of a socially determined exchange value to which individual value judgments adjust themselves"? [11] On the contrary, it is Pesch's claim that he has given to price theory "a formula which considers the influence of the individual evaluation on the price without neglecting those objective factors which in conjunction with it determine the formation of prices" (V, 33–34). Not only is the general evaluation not independent of individual evaluations, but it has its origin in the judgments of the individuals. It could not be otherwise for it is the individual use value of a good which constitutes the motive of every exchange. Every buyer and seller profits in exchange because the individual use value of the good which

[11] Harris thus criticizes Pesch, *op. cit.*, p. 44.

he obtains is greater to him than the use value of the good which he must give up. Without this there would be no exchange.

And Pesch states explicitly: "The individual evaluation influences the general evaluation and measurement of the exchange value and price, according to this general evaluation, and indeed in a distinctive way." (V, 40). His explanation how the individual evaluation affects the general, akin to the scholastic epistemological analysis of the origin of the universal concept, manifests his broad philosophical background. Within the personal economic sphere the value of a good is individualized according to concrete, particular conditions. In its wanderings in the market-place this value is generalized; it steps out of the individual sphere and serves as the basis of the evaluation not only of a particular individual but of a group.

> Yet the individual evaluation does not merely flow along with the general evaluation. On the contrary it has causal significance for the formation and mutations of the general evaluation and market prices (*ibid.*).

When it is a question of the personal desires of many, certain universal objective forces are found at work: the need and desire of many directed toward the same type of good.

> The individual as a particular disappears in the mass, but in the determination of that which is common or similar it co-operates in the social evaluation. The individual as such is absorbed in the joint action. What remains as the object of the evaluation is the good with its usefulness for the average conditions and its quantity circumstances in relation to the general need of this circle of persons and economies participating in the exchange market (V, 41).[12]

---

[12] Cf. Marshall: "He (the economist) studies rather 'the course of action that may be expected under certain conditions from the members of an industrial group,' in so far as the motives of that action are measurable by a money price; and in these broad results the variety and the fickleness of *individual* action are

It should be noted that the general evaluation is not the sum of the individual evaluations. Rather this social evaluation represents the result of their combination and agreement. But, "the individual evaluation has still cooperated in the formation of this agreement," and the particular circumstances influence the general evaluation in so far as it depends on the income of the buyers (*ibid.*). (See also V, 17–19.)

The price established by these objective factors via the individual judgments merging into the *communis aestimatio* is still a datum for the individual in the market. "The market price appears to the individual as something objective, which he cannot change" (V, 38). Also, it is recognized by Pesch that this price is not established *a priori* but experimentally "by a continual probing this way and that" (V, 37). Moreover, "the general evaluation does not lead to a mathematically precise establishment of exchange value and price" (V, 51). The market price presents a certain range.

But, is there a place for the cost of production in the framework of Pesch's value theory? The cost of production [13] under normal conditions will be an external measure of the price. It is called the "regulator of the price"; and in a certain sense in practice represents the normal price. Demand and supply are not excluded here; they determine the price for a particular time and place. But this temporary price fluctuates

---

merged in the comparatively regular *aggregate* of the action of many" (*Principles of Economics, op. cit.*, p. 98). (Parentheses and italics added.)

[13] Production costs here are taken to be "average, general, socially necessary costs, i.e., such costs which according to the social status of production technique, of the business organization, of the productivity of labor must be applied, . . . thus not the individual cost of a single producer" (V, 32).

Costs in general are defined: "The sum of exchange value, which is expended . . . for the attaining, the manufacturing, the production of an economic good" (V, 21).

"Opportunity" cost, which Pesch considers important for a national economic analysis, in relation to the firm is called "provisional" or "hypothetical" cost. The latter expressions he applies to Wieser's definition of production cost as "the amount of means of production which are required for a particular product and thus must be withdrawn from another product" (V, 22).

around a long-run normal dependent on the cost of production. Pesch even uses the expression "the law of production costs," whereby the price of goods whose production is limited swings around the highest cost of production; and the price of goods whose production can be expanded "indefinitely" swings around the lowest production cost (V, 32).

Nevertheless, Pesch holds that cost does not immediately establish the value of the product. Value is immediately determined by utility and scarcity. However, if scarcity is described as "difficulty of acquirement," then it can both signify sparseness in relation to the demand and can refer to the cost of production. But the latter does not directly affect the price, but only indirectly in so far as it influences the supply. "It (the cost of production) determines the value not 'immediately' but 'mediately' and 'materially' . . ." (V, 31).

A confirmation that the competitive price is the optimum is found in Pesch's exposition of the "morally" just price.[14] The moral "ought" is proposed as the economic "should be." The goal of the economy, he reasons, can be achieved only by a suitable production, income, and price pattern. But income and price can contribute to the fulfillment of this task only if they are founded on justice. And the price which conforms to this requirement of justice is the competitive price (V, 93–4).

This is not a forced conclusion for on analysis it is clear that the same factors required for the establishment of a just price are also the determinants of the competitive price. "We find in this theory (the Scholastic doctrine of just price) the combination of 'subjective' and 'objective' factors has exercised decisive influence on the formation of prices . . ." (V, 90). The parallelism of requirements is easily shown, for

[14] Cf. Oswald v. Nell-Breuning's exposition of the just price, based on Pesch, "The Concept of the Just Price," *Review of Social Economy*, VIII (September, 1950), pp. 111–22.

the demands of a just price are that the price must correspond to the value of the goods exchanged, and it must offer a return measured by the labor and expended cost.

1. The exchange of goods requires an equivalent return for both sides, *"aequalitas rei ad rem,"* equality of exchange value. Exchanging and buying belong to the *"contractus non gratuiti."* They offer a profit for both sides in so far as the one requires the thing of the other. Both sides gain by the exchange; but they should not gain in the sense of doing so by means of the price, so that the agreement of prices with exchange value is abandoned.

The determination of exchange value depends on the evaluation. In the market the individual evaluation is not decisive, but the general evaluation which measures the exchange value according to the need of the community. The price can change *"secundum diversitatem loci et temporis,"* since the general evaluation does not form the same estimate for all times and places.

2. Justice requires a return corresponding to the cost, which holds for the wages of labor, the undertaking of effort, risk, etc. The two requirements stand in complete agreement. They are not contradictory. The one does not exclude the other requirement of exchange justice. The product is provided in the exchange, and for this product an equivalent return is required. The cost finds its remuneration precisely through the fact that the product has a value to which such a price is due. A profit is allowed; it may not however be derived from the transgression of the just price (V, 87–88).

2. The Peschian Paradox: Divergence from the Competitive Optimum

A possible divergence from the optimum price is acknowledged by both Pesch and the conventional theorist. The classical example of deviation is the case of monopoly. According to conventional theory, in monopoly marginal cost does not equal price and thus results a malallocation of resources. In Peschian terms, monopoly price does not conform to the true exchange value, or the objective factors. The problem, he explains, is that cost of production is not necessarily a decisive factor in the determination of the monopoly price; and there is no guarantee that the whole of a useful product will be available to the nation. The latter means:

> The competitive price is decisive by virtue of its distribution function only in determining who will use the good. The monopolist can bring it about that no one uses it (V, 54).

The monopolist may seek his profit not by increasing the favorable factor, utility, but by increasing the unfavorable factor, scarcity.

Except for the discord in their explanations of what this divergence signifies—based on their different approach in value theory—there is no argument here between the conventional theorist and Pesch. Moreover, they both will admit that in the real world even under competition the market at every moment is not in equilibrium. But here the important issue arises, about which they do differ: Does the competitive system tend toward equilibrium or toward disequilibrium and an ultimate monopolistic or oligopolistic situation?

Pesch's answer to this question introduces what may be called the Peschian paradox. For, while he contends that the competitive price is the optimum, he also asserts that free competition leads to a divergence from this optimum. Two important questions are of concern in this connection: (1) Is it true that free competition leads to a divergence from the optimum? (2) Independent of the former question, are there other reasons why free competition is desirable?

An example of the conventional position that competition

tends toward the competitive equilibrium may be taken from George F. Stigler's representative textbook, *The Theory of Competitive Price*. Discussing Pigou's threefold division of equilibrium, the author comments:

> It is simple to concoct artificial economic situations in which neutral and unstable equilibriums exist, but in price theory concerned with real phenomena these cases are highly exceptional. A few cases of unstable equilibrium will be noted subsequently, but the conditions necessary to stable equilibrium (called the *stability* conditions) are usually fulfilled.[15]

A Peschian paraphrase of this would be: It is simple to concoct artificial economic situations in which stable equilibrium exists, but in price theory concerned with real phenomena these cases are highly exceptional. Absolute free competition, according to Pesch, leads to anarchy in the market place, that is, to overproduction, an exaggerated fall in prices, crises, and economic ruin. And the ultimate result is monopoly.

> As long as competition increases and betters the product, lowers the price to the limit of the cost of production, it operates profitably for the consumer. If, however, through reckless battle, it lessens the number of producers it is ultimately dangerous for the consumer. It leads then to artificial monopoly (V, 55; see also III, 388, 391–92).

This tendency of competition to degenerate into monopoly is not viewed as an accidental phenomenon but as a logical consequent of competition's self-interest postulate.

> Under the rule of the free competitive system the competitor's endeavor aims at being as much as possible free from competition. In order to secure, to increase their own enterprise profit,

15 George F. Stigler, *The Theory of Competitive Price* (New York: Macmillan, 1942), p. 27. (Italics in original.)

the burdensome competitors must be eliminated, destroyed. This precisely "free" competition permits (IV, 258).[16]

The means listed which free competition employs to achieve this elimination present a catalogue of what we have come to know as the standard practices of monopolistic competition: place advantage, patent rights, advertising, styles, particular retail practices, etc.

In his conspectus of the "law of production costs" for the case of an "indefinitely" multipliable product Pesch surveys the transition from competition to monopoly. Following Adolph Wagner he distinguishes three phases.

In the first stage even the individual cost which is necessary to fill the demand works determinately on the price. Supposing different enterprises with different production costs, "so long as the market demand can only barely be covered by the total production of all the enterprises the price will thus be determined by the highest production cost which must be expended for the last part of the marginal supply which is still necessary to cover the market demand" (V, 32). This brings to the producers with lower costs a profit, a differential-rent, which increases their capital power and has influential repercussions in the subsequent stages.

In the second phase of the development takes place the expansion of the more favorably situated enterprises and the displacement of the competition of the less favorably situated. On the principle that generally with increased sales production costs will be lower, prices are lowered by the producers with lower costs. They now have a greater share of the market

16 For a very interesting and competent article defending this same thesis, see M. M. Bober, "Economic Assumptions and Monopoly," in *Explorations in Economics* (New York: McGraw-Hill, 1936), pp. 336–45; also, J. M. Clark's reference to "unmitigated competition" which "so often goes (or used to go) to ruinous cutthroat lengths, driving the participants into various kinds of protective arrangements" ("Financing High-Level Employment," in *Financing American Prosperity, op. cit.,* p. 122).

and greater profits, and also have abundant credits, etc., at their disposal. The higher cost producer will be able to sell at the lower price only at a loss.

In the third and final stage the large firm is victorious over a wide area. It has available better techniques and receives greater profits from the lowering of costs. However, it sweeps the independent enterprise out of business and "thus another economically (even for the formation of price) less favorable result follows upon this development" (V, 33).

Manifestly, Pesch's assumption of decreasing costs apparently over a considerable range of the firm's cost function and the assumption of difficulty of entry which becomes cumulatively more difficult eliminates any possibility of attaining even the pure competition solution, let alone that of perfect competition. But what about the more realistic competition position which acknowledges—besides other imperfections—possible decreasing costs and barriers to freedom of entry? The basic variant separating Pesch from the pure but realistic competition theorist is expressed most clearly in Galbraith's excellent description of the fundamental difference between Mr. Sraffa and his contemporaries when his famous article appeared in the *Economic Journal* in 1926. One could very well substitute the name of "Pesch" for "Sraffa" in the following long but appropriate quotation.

> Subject to qualifications, the tendency at the time Mr. Sraffa's article appeared was to recognize the limiting case of monopoly, but to assume, in general, a rule of competition. Competition was not assumed to be perfect. Those already in the business might variously obstruct the entry of newcomers. Or entry might be rendered difficult by the prestige associated with trademarks and trade names. Imperfect knowledge of opportunities might interfere. Decreasing costs were deemed an especially serious handicap for the newcomer, who, because he was new, was likely to be small. If large scale and accom-

panying requirements in capital and organization brought
substantial economies, the small newcomer was faced with an
organic handicap. Nevertheless, these barriers, though widely
recognized, were conventionally assumed to be of secondary
effect. They were frictions that muddied and at times diverted
but did not check the great underlying current which was
toward a competitive equilibrium. Given that equilibrium,
there was a presumption, again subject to many dissenting
voices, that economic resources would be employed with maximum efficiency and the product so distributed as to maximize
satisfactions. Sraffa attacked the assumption that the "frictions" were in fact a secondary and fugitive phenomenon. He
argued they were stable and indeed cumulative and yielded a
solution consistent not with a competitive, but a monopolistic
equilibrium. He argued that monopoly, not free competition,
was the more appropriate assumption in market theory.[17]

Pesch, too, would contend that free competition is not the
appropriate assumption in market theory. For, he claims,
"free price formation has become a phantom" (V, 57). And
it is his belief that in the Germany of the twenties "almost
every industry has become cartelized in some form" (III, 259).

It might be too readily assumed that Pesch's theory of competition leading to disequilibrium and to a state of monopoly
is nothing else than Marx's "law of concentration." Indeed,
there is great similarity between the two positions; but they
are not identical. According to the Marxian doctrine this
concentration is necessary and general and is due to the private
ownership of the means of production which engenders business crisis. Pesch denies concentration is a general phenomenon, pointing particularly to agriculture and certain segments
of industry which are more profitable on a small scale. Moreover, a limit to the optimum of concentration is recognized
because of the increased risk due to the greater capital in-

---

[17] J. K. Galbraith, "Monopoly and the Concentration of Economic Power,"
in *A Survey of Contemporary Economics, op. cit.*, pp. 99–100.

vestment and the taking over of entrepreneurial functions by managing officials (IV, 551–52; see also I, 384–86). The concentration of industry which has taken place—and Pesch admits the increased tendency following World War I—is held to be due not to the private ownership of the means of production, but to the anarchy created by "absolute free competition, the atomistic tendency of economic individualism" (I, 383–84).[18]

The solution of the Peschian value paradox should now be clear. The price realized in the competitive market is the optimum, and as long as the market structure remains unchanged no major divergence from the optimum will take place. However, Pesch expects that given a certain time period the market structure will not remain unchanged. Perhaps we may say that viewed statically competition yields the optimum price, but viewed dynamically competition, because it ceases to be competition, leads to a divergence. And here the dynamic is the more realistic and more significant assumption.

Before discussing other market forms, such as bilateral monopoly and cartels (oligopoly), it is important to return to the second question asked above: even if competition leads to a divergence from the optimum, are there benefits to be derived from competition? The answer has significance for policy because, if benefits exist, obviously they should be retained as much as possible, though other harmful competitive features must be eliminated or regulated. In unhesitating terms Pesch explicitly acknowledges the benefits due to competition: "We owe to free competitive enterprise the great benefits of the last century in the field of knowledge and 'know-how'; in it dwells a never failing, animated, creative force; it is able to harness the forces for the highest production, always creating new goods for the welfare of the people" (IV, 220–21).[19]

[18] Pesch does not overlook the credit he feels is due to Marx, for he admits: "No one saw as clearly as Marx the absurdity of an arbitrary dominion of property and of this 'anarchy' of purely private economic production" (IV, 206).
[19] "Should we not, under the circumstances, therefore, try not for 'pure'

If Pesch can write in such complimentary fashion of the benefits of competition and still repudiate its evils so strongly, it is evident that he recognizes two kinds of competition: a beneficial and harmful competition. The former is called "sound" competition; the latter "free" (not a sufficiently distinctive term), "reckless," "unbridled," or "absolute" competition.[20]

In the Peschian categories of market forms bilateral monopoly is not an unwelcome appendage—as so often in modern price theory—but is afforded a prominent function. Prior to *Competition Among the Few* [21] bilateral monopoly and oligopoly were usually relegated to the appendices. It being reasoned, explicitly or implicitly, that such markets offered only indeterminate solutions, while the main body of price theory was concerned with determinate equilibria.[22]

It is true that in Pesch bilateral monopoly has not as prominent a place as found in Fellner, but there is presented the framework for such a treatment. Bilateral monopoly price is conceived as analogous to the "conventional price" of individual exchange where a general evaluation is lacking and the decision about the exchange value is arrived at by bargaining in view of "the objective good qualities and scarcity of the object exchanged" (V, 53). It is a question of a product desired

---

competition but for 'workable' competition? Our reason for doing so will not so much be to meet mathematical standards of optimum output as to preserve the technological creativeness and personal democracy of our social structure" (David McCord Wright, "The Prospects for Capitalism," in *A Survey of Contemporary Economics, op. cit.*, p. 467).

20 "What must be stressed . . . is that some kinds of competition are good and some kinds are bad. It should be possible for economics even without soiling its scientific objectivity, to throw some light on which is which. . . . It is evident that as economists we are faced with the necessity of a thorough re-examination of the theory of competition, with a view to providing a useful framework for subsequent value judgments" (Kenneth E. Boulding [Discussion], "Recent Anti-Trust Decisions," *American Economic Review*, XXXIX [May, 1949], pp. 320–21).

21 William Fellner, *Competition Among the Few* (New York: Knopf, 1949).
22 *Ibid.*, p. 9.

by a few—and Pesch believes that such goods are on the whole rather numerous. "There are certainly innumerable grada-tions between scarce goods in the proper sense and mass-production articles" (V, 52). An important aspect of this market of a few is that price is accepted as "the expression of the mutually recognized exchange value" (V, 53).[23]

Pesch calls explicit attention to the analogy between indi-vidual exchange and bilateral monopoly:

> The price battle today takes place frequently between closely united warring lords, buying and selling cartels. It is a question here about an analogy to the isolated, individual exchange, where one buyer is opposed to one seller (conven-tional price!). Similarly it is true about the wage battle be-tween organized employers and employees (*ibid.*, note).

Again, this analysis has important implications for policy. Because of the widespread activities of cartels, Pesch looks to the organization of consumers in order to bring about an "equality of power" and to give the consumer greater influence in the determination of price (V, 55). Thus he suggests the uncommon solution for the non-competitive market problem, the establishment of bilateral monopolies.

It would be difficult to understand Pesch's treatment of prices and markets (or that of any German economist) without a consideration of his views on cartels. For in Germany more than any other leading industrial country the cartel was a representative form of market organization; there it was given

---

[23] Speaking of bilateral monopoly, Fellner concludes: "Shifting from an agreement by which joint profits are *not* maximized to an agreement by which they *are* maximized always makes possible an increase in the profits of *each* participant. Therefore a tendency toward joint profit maximization should be expected here . . ." (*ibid.*, p. 247). This conclusion is qualified by Fellner, however, if consideration is taken of attempts to secure safety margins against less favorable outcomes than appear probable; long-run objectives of the firms; the existence of controlling groups in the firms, and the adoption of cutthroat policies or the desire to avoid them. These qualifications, however, apply also to other markets besides bilateral monopoly.

legal status.[24] It has significance for American economists since our economy is characterized by the prevalence of monopoly, oligopoly with or without trade agreements, and price leadership—market forms very similar to cartels.[25] To the American mind the word "cartel" usually signifies something sinister, chiefly because cartels have contacted our economic life through international cartels, one of the termini of which has often operated secretly and illegally in view of our antitrust laws.

Cartels are defined by Pesch:

> Freely stipulated arrangements or combinations of independent enterprises created by free agreements, usually for a definite period of time, for the purpose of keeping remote the evils of anarchistic production and limitless competition through the regulation of production and sales by a sufficient control of markets (III, 356).

The essential goal of the cartel is protection from anarchistic production, the evil of limitless competition. The means is the regulation of production and markets. And this requires a limitation of competition and the concomitant rise of monopoly. However, not an absolute but a relative monopoly position is essential to the idea of a cartel (III, 357, 370).[26]

In the realm of production and costs the cartel is seen to offer many possible benefits. Production can be more steady than under free competition; crisis can be dampened. And though *de facto* many abuses exist in the application of pro-

[24] For a brief history of cartels, see III, pp. 377–86. For a brief account in English of the history of the German cartels, see Gustav Stolper, *German Economy 1870–1940* (New York: Reynal & Hitchcock, 1940), pp. 83–88, 209–10.

[25] "So-called cartel agreements differ from the quasi-agreements here considered (of oligopoly) in that they involve explicit agreement. . . . The analytical framework suitable for the discussion of cartel problems is not fundamentally different from that developed in the preceding pages (dealing with oligopolistic quasi-agreements)." (William Fellner, *op. cit.*, pp. 229–30.) (Parentheses added.)

[26] For the difference between a monopoly and cartel, according to Pesch, see III, 363–64.

duction to consumer needs, still the possibility of a suitable application exists. Lower costs are possible from the protection from crisis, which lowers capital risk. Also, the demand is more accurately known; advertising costs can be reduced.[27] And competition is now shifted from the field of price to the technical sphere. With price given, the entrepreneur seeks ways and means of lowering cost. And though in the long run it is impossible to carry weak members, still in the short run such members may be given time to correct, if possible, their cost structure (III, 386–91).

The major disadvantage of cartels, on the other hand, is the possibility that they will set excessively high prices. However, Pesch reasons that the price will be lower than that established by the survivors or survivor of the competitive battle. Moreover, the price theoretically could be lower than the competitive price because "dead costs" such as advertising can be eliminated.[28] The possibility of an excessively high price is a proximate danger where the cartel position approaches the absolute monopoly case in which the cartelized enterprises have exclusive control over a product, e.g., coal, petroleum, potash, etc. Where such an absolute monopoly position is not acquired many hindrances may restrain the cartel. Potential or latent competition, domestic or foreign, must be considered. Also, high prices may make production

[27] "A large degree of monopoly is often urged as the best instrument for prevention or cure of over-investment. In this there is some logic. When firms are few, with or without agreement, each is probably able to assess supply and demand conditions better than when sellers are much more numerous, and each has a greater incentive to do so since his policy will affect appreciably the conditions in the whole market." (Donald H. Wallace, "Monopolistic Competition and Public Policy," *American Economic Review*, XXVI, Supplement [March, 1936], p. 84; reprinted in *Readings in the Social Control of Industry*, p. 274.) Wallace points out, however, that a large degree of monopoly power, if not successfully regulated, can bring even worse results in the matter of overinvestment.

[28] Obviously, here the competitive price is not that of pure competition but of monopolistic competition.

quotas irksome. Or, the fear of weakening demand or of consumers turning to substitutes, perhaps establishing their own production, tends to keep the cartel price reasonable.

But what of the broader benefits of competition, in particular, initiative, technical progress and economic freedom? Pesch believes one can "rightly prescind" from the question of initiative since it is not attached to the "unbridled" competition cartels seek to eliminate (III, 390, note 2). Nor, in his opinion, is there any less freedom in the monopoly of a cartel than in the monopoly of a plutocracy to which unlimited competition leads. Recognized as a real danger, though, is cartel domination of raw material producers and distributors. But the chief complaint is that submerged battles are intensified because of their collective character. Competition is now between giant organizations, the effects of whose acts are certain to be of the greatest consequence for the whole community. "Organized economic spheres stand opposed to organized economic spheres . . ." (III, 404).[29]

Also condemned by Pesch is the spirit of individualism underlying the battle of the giants, which is manifested in their conflicts with their own members, unions, agricultural groups, consumers, and against each other. What is needed is a practical acceptance of the principle of solidarity—otherwise every coalition based on self-interest alone becomes "more potent individualism" (III, 404).

To sum up in the words of Pesch:

> There is presented as the economically suitable goal not the suppression of competition . . . but the regulation of com-

[29] "This spirit of irresponsible self-seeking persisted into a new age in which the competitive checks are vanishing or being progressively weakened, and in which group organization is taking the place of the competing individual. These group organizations have power, for good or for harm, which the simple individual did not possess" (J. M. Clark, "Educational Functions of Economics after the War," *American Economic Review*, XXXIV, Proceedings [March, 1944], p. 64).

petition; not the exploitation of the consumer, but the ensuring of a fair price. In so far as cartels are suited to diminish or to overcome in this sense the dangers and damage of the anarchistic state of production and competition, they may be welcomed as an economically useful type of organization. But, as we saw, at the same time certainly the practical prospective possibility of a refining process must be assumed *vis-à-vis* the tendency which is inclined to find in such organizations the means of every practice of monopolistic growth, especially of unduly increasing price and profit (III, 406).

3. Price Policy

As the immediate goal of price policy economists of all shades—the conventional theorist, the socialist, and Heinrich Pesch—are in accord in postulating the ideal of the competitive price. However, one difference between Pesch and the other two groups exists in that, because of his deeper theoretical treatment of value, the former can reformulate his goal in terms of seeking the most general objective evaluation.[30] The significance of this variant approach, which is not inconsequential, comes to light in the means proposed to implement the goal.

To realize the ideal of the competitive price, a few "pure" theorists (e.g., Hayek) recommend the restoration of competition. By the more moderate price theorist (e.g., Clark, Ellis) the attainment of a "workable" competition is suggested. Even for some Socialists the *desideratum* is the setting up of the competitive mechanism in the framework of state ownership. Pesch's general means is the establishment of order in the price system.

[30] The importance of this broader formulation is clear from Professor Chamberlin's introduction of a heterogeneous product into the welfare norm. See his "Product Heterogeneity and Public Policy," *op. cit.,* pp. 84–85.

The self-imposed limited recommendation of pure theory is required because without an analysis of what the market value really represents its policy program can only seek to establish the reality of the assumptions of pure competitive theory. But, what if it is impossible to realize these assumptions? As Galbraith so decisively puts it: ". . . the norm of pure competition, however valuable as an intellectual design or model, provides few practical clues to action *vis-à-vis* markets where the possibility of such competition is rejected." [31] To realize Hayek's perfect competitive world "would take some of the most formidable planning (and one of the largest bureaucracies) of all time." [32] The socialist solution, inasmuch as it is conditioned on the establishment of government ownership of the means of production, will be a more pertinent question for a later chapter. The program of moderate pure theorists will be found to be in general accord, though with a difference of emphasis, with Pesch's proposals. However, it seems that the latter is able to offer a more considered *rationale* for his recommendations.

The Peschian regulating factors to implement the establishment of order in the market are the triumvirate: the individual (producers and consumers), the state, and vocational groups.

The individual producer by a more comprehensive study of market conditions will be able to eliminate waste and to create articles more valuable for the consumers (IV, 174, 184). Major benefits are hoped for, if a new spirit will inspire the producer to seek his profit in the creation of new utility rather than in a difference between price and real exchange value, and to consider the welfare of the nation above his subjective, private gain (IV, 180, 188).

For the consumer a more effective voice in the determina-

[31] J. K. Galbraith, *op. cit.*, p. 104. The discussion here of Arthur R. Burns' difficulties when he rejected pure competition as an impractical goal is quite instructive.

[32] *Ibid.*, p. 111, note 29.

tion of price must be attained. Pesch says the important question is: whether and how the consumer is to have a voice in the prices set by the secret price agreements of producers (V, 57)? The consumer is no longer willing merely "to read" prices as a "given," prices which he knows are not the result of inexorable economic laws, but are the effects of human forces and power (IV, 167). Pesch hopes to see established more consumer organizations which will cooperate in price determination by placing organized buyers opposite organized sellers (V, 56). The same reasoning would apply here as is made in the labor market, where a single employer or employer organization stands opposed to unorganized workers. In such a market the wage (or price) can hardly be expected to reflect the objective factors involved.

Among consumers, also, a redirection of spirit is called for. They must not seek always to buy the cheapest priced goods, but must be more conscious of the "fair" price, which respects the legitimate profit of the producer and corresponds to the requirements of an economically sound providing for needs (IV, 196).

The role of the state in the price determination problem is an important one, especially where the vocational groups are wanting. It would be erroneous, however, because of Pesch's emphasis on the objectivity of exchange value (though the subjective factors were no wise neglected), to conclude that he favors compulsory prices, whether fixed by the state or vocational groups. As he explicitly states:

> He, who has followed our explanation carefully, cannot escape from the fact that according to our system general evaluation, high as we consider its importance, still has no compulsory character. Moreover, we presume a free exchange economy without official price regulation (V, 51–52).

Pesch realizes the practical difficulties in the way of setting official prices and he does not recommend it. Nevertheless, he cannot refrain from commenting on the fact that "because of the division of the non-organized consumer, without official prices the necessary means of life are set too high for them" (V, 56; see IV, 223–24).

The Peschian presentation of the state's role in regard to competition reveals a different emphasis from that of conventional economics. Reflecting his analysis of competition as leading to a divergence from the optimum his watchword, rather than the conventional "restoration of competition," is the "regulation of competition." He does admit, however, that political laws and authority should not unnecessarily limit competitive business—the employment of special knowledge, skill, inventions, nor a sound freedom of competitive business (IV, 220). And while in time of war monopolies may be necessary, in peace time the condition of freedom for industry, especially for trade is perceived as a need. But it is asked: "Must therefore the principle of absolute freedom of trade be introduced into economic life?" (IV, 228). His answer:

> He, who knows no other model for the organization of the economy than the two extremes of monopoly and free competition, will be inclined to let free competition in its absolute sense take the place of monopoly. A rational economic policy, on the contrary, does not forget that a regulation of freedom even without monopoly is possible and within proper limits is necessarily desired for the public welfare of the people (*ibid.*).

In many respects one of the most knotty problems for the conventional economist who rejects philosophic knowledge or who holds to a philosophy of individualism is the question of the legitimate and proper policy of the state in regard to monopoly and particularly oligopoly. Pesch, too, in his discussion of the analogous cartel, must admit: "State regulation of cartels remains in the long run indispensable; it is of the highest importance, but of no less difficulty" (III, 394). His social philosophy, however, enables him to lessen the number of problems facing the individualistic economist. The right to organize is acknowledged as a fundamental right of man. It exists before the state, indeed, is the original foundation of the state itself. Yet the state may limit the exercise of this right.

> If consequently the state is not the sovereign lord and master of the citizens' associations in the sense that it may suppress and arbitrarily limit the right to organize, it still has the right to regulate the exercise of this right in order to check abuses, to prevent harmful combinations, to stimulate and further the useful, to require what is necessary (III, 343).

The application of this social principle is much in order in respect to cartels, as Pesch readily recognizes.

> The practical importance of such a political regulation of the exercise of the right to organize is evident. . . . Unfortunately experience proves only too often that every combination of organized interests easily operates in a one-sided way, does not always bear a proper sympathy towards the interests of others nor even of the community interest (*ibid.*).

Nor would Pesch claim that it is an easy task to set the proper limit so that both the community interests and those of the particular groups are served. He admits simply: "Without compromise it will not come about" (*ibid.*).

In the realm of practical policy, according to Pesch, cartels (*mutatis mutandis* oligopoly and monopoly) cannot be suppressed without the loss of the benefits they afford. But what must be eliminated are the setting of excessively high prices and the misuse of their centralized, monopolistic power against buyers, independent enterprises, members of the cartel, and the workers (III, 395; IV, 554).

In his opinion a general law to establish norms for the regulation of cartels is not practical.[33] The chief difficulty

---

[33] However, "Particular laws for individual industries or articles (e.g., steel, coal) can consider better the peculiarities of these fields" (III, 397).

centers around the issue of price determination which gives rise to many perplexing questions. What body shall decide about the price: a judge, congress, or a special board of all the interested parties? And since it is not easy to consider all the objective and subjective factors coming into play, how is the fairness of the price to be measured? Also how will the decisions be carried out: by setting fixed prices or maximum prices? He suggests in the case of a notorious abuse of the monopoly position, and if other regulations do not avail, that direct price control be interposed—the establishment of price maxima. For the just price is "a difficult but not an impossible concept" (III, 398).

But it is only in exceptional cases and for particular problems that a direct intervention by the state is recommended. To nationalize a cartelized industry would be more than direct intervention and would be justified only in extreme need (III, 400).

Normally an indirect procedure is recommended before either direct intervention, such as price control or nationalization. To this pertains: (1) publicity—cartel registration; (2) control by a cartel bureau; (3) proper disposition of the tariff policy; (4) proper regulation of transportation costs; (5) political fostering of organizations opposed to the cartels and of competitors independent of the cartels—by favorable taxation policy, preference to non-cartelized industries in public purchases, etc. (III, 399–400).

The final means to bring order into the price system is the vocational group. In fact, one of the bright sides of the cartel picture for Pesch is that "the present day cartels are transition forms; they render pioneer service, preparing for the formation of more perfect forms" (III, 401). The terminus of this transition is the corporative association. He expresses the possibility that World War I with its unfortunate economic consequences may have "accelerated a development by which 'social evaluating organs' (vocational organizations) can again assert their influence on the formation of prices in new and more universal forms" (V, 57). And it is recommended in order to arrive at a more general objective valuation that "organizations be created within which producers, middlemen, and consumers have a voice" (V, 93). It should be noted that in these vocational organizations compulsion is not a characteristic; it is the last means to be used, and only when the general welfare requires it (see IV, 539).

MONETARY THEORY

Heinrich Pesch's monetary theory is closely related to his general value theory. Dominated by the same teleological approach, stressing again both the objective and subjective aspects of the problem, monetary theory is explicitly set in the framework of general value theory. The concern is primarily with fundamental questions. What is money? What constitutes the value of money? How is the value of money determined?

The importance of money for the economy is recognized, but a mercantilistic overemphasis of this importance is rejected. "Though money is not everything in the economy, still it is of great importance" (V, 131). It is his opinion that it is erroneous to believe that without money an economy with a division of labor and a system of exchange would be impossible. However, an advanced and complicated system of exchange and division of labor presupposes the use of money. Likewise, he seeks to avoid the classical and mathematical schools' "neutrality" approach to the place of money in economic theory.

His opposition to mercantilism and his pointed emphasis on labor as the source of wealth had led Adam Smith to see in money merely "the great wheel of circulation, the great instrument of commerce" from which one can usually prescind in economic research; indeed in order to evaluate exchange transactions one must concentrate directly on all the processes without reference to money. Against this position it must again be maintained that, while he may still abstract from money in much of his theoretical study, nevertheless the economist can no more forget the actual influence of money on the phenomena and circumstances of economic life than the physicist who in theory assumes a vacuum may deny or overlook the influence of air on the actual movements of bodies (V, 130–31).

1. The Nature of Money

A useful aid to comprehend the notion of money is to reflect on its origin. Unacceptable to Pesch is the rationalistic "formal contract" which, similar to its political science counterpart, the "social contract" theory of the origin of the state, seeks to explain the introduction of money into the economy by an explicit formal agreement. Like Aristotle, Pesch views the use of money as a natural process arising from the difficulties of barter and the desire for a satisfactory measure of value.

Two distinct senses of the term "money" are basic in Pesch's discussion of the concept of money. In the juridical sense, money is legal tender; it embraces whatever the state proclaims to be money. Here the means of payment function is emphasized. In the economic sense, money is whatever is accepted in trade—this seems to be the more popular concept in recent Anglo-American literature. These two basic concepts are distinct, but frequently overlap. For example, today in the mind of the public money is whatever the state calls money. But the state might make paper money legal tender which in extraordinary times through a lack of confidence the public would refuse to accept. In this case the paper money would be money in the juridical sense, not, however, in the economic sense. Or, perhaps it should be called "inferior" or "false" money (V, 165–70).

Combining the juridical and economic sense, money is defined as:

> A means of exchange and payment suitable for the comparison and transference of value, whose employment for these purposes is introduced and ordered within a definite area by public authority and with legal responsibility, and which has found general acceptance and validity (V, 171).

This recognition of the juridical aspect of money does not involve Pesch in the acceptance of Knapp's state theory of money. On the contrary his recognition and distinction of the juridical element enables him to indicate the incompleteness of Knapp's purely juridical approach. Pesch admits that juridically the state can and does create money; nominally it can order anything to be money and can invest it with the character of money. But the state cannot create economic value. Ultimately the legal title bestowed on money by the state is not the decisive factor determining its exchange value. Any system which seeks to clothe the state with a certain absolutism in the creation of money must be rejected. For the state has obligations and if it fails to recognize them it will be an evil day for the monetary system (V, 164, 167, 210–11).

As in all definitions of money, the Peschian, given above, reveals the functions considered essential to the concept of money. Four functions are mentioned and it is believed that all must be fulfilled before anything can be called "money" in the complete sense. Money serves as (1) a general means of value-comparison and price determination; (2) a general means of exchange; (3) a means of payment; (4) a store of value (a means of storing and transporting value) (V, 132).

Some attention to his commentary on these functions may be helpful to understand Pesch's concept of money. The basic function is considered to be the comparison of value, for "only on the supposition that prices can be expressed in monetary terms is the means of exchange function possible and understandable" (V, 135). To be a measure of value money must itself be an object of value, just as a pound weight is required to measure the weight of an object, and an ounce container is needed to measure an ounce of a liquid. Economic value can only be measured by an economic good. This does not mean that all money must necessarily have its own proper material value. It is admitted that in the modern economy paper money is playing an increasingly prominent role. However, paper money is still expressed in terms of marks, schillings, etc., and behind the paper money even when nonconvertible will be found metallic money possessing its own proper value.

This standard-of-value function is not considered by Pesch as that of an abstract unit of account, the view of some modern writers on the subject. He says explicitly: ". . . money is not an abstract unit of value, but a concrete means of payment" (V, 170). And elsewhere he explains that if today money is employed as an abstract unit of account, it is only because a concrete monetary system existed prior to this. "Whether a compensatory system without a real money base would have developed in this way, if the money were only an abstract unit of account, may very well be doubted" (V, 266). And he points out that fundamentally such a monetary theory lacks every economic point of view and every socio-legal foundation without which there can hardly be an economic or monetary theory.

The means-of-exchange function is likened to a "switching

station." Ultimately this round-about way is shorter than direct exchange, because in the latter case a coincidence of wants may be lacking. In the performance of this exchange function even metallic money appears only as a means of exchange, its commodity quality recedes into the background (V, 135).

The means-of-payment function is mentioned to provide for the cases falling outside exchange transactions in the strict sense. This function includes the payment of debts and taxes, the bestowing of gifts, the establishing of foundations, and also, the payment of wages (for labor is not a commodity). When the notion of obligatory acceptance is introduced the function of money as a means of payment rests on the legal authority which proclaims it legal tender.

The function of a store of value is thought to follow immediately from the means-of-payment function (V, 171, note 1). A time and place function are involved here. As a store of value —with hoarding one of the important elements—the reference is to time. The place reference is called a "transference of value" (V, 136).

The significance of a proper concept of money and its functions emerges in the practical problem of which monetary standard is to be adopted. Should a metallic or paper standard be adopted? Because metallic money more easily inspires the confidence of the people and thus becomes generally accepted Pesch prefers a metallic standard. A free coinage and an elastic system of credit is favored as the best means to supply a reliable circulating media adaptable to changing needs (V, 264). Pesch is no rigid defender of the gold standard, being well aware that gold offers no absolute guarantee of stability (V, 255). But it is to be preferred until a more suitable metal is available.

The leading opponents of the gold standard, the nominalists, claim in their chartalist theory that money is a creation of the state and its sole function is to act as a unit of account. Logically, this concept of money leads to the advocacy of a paper standard. Gold in this case is to be used solely to balance foreign exchange transactions or to be accumulated in the central reserve, even though the circulating paper money is not to be convertible into gold (V, 258).

While he repudiates the false theories on which its recommendation is based, Pesch, like Smith and Ricardo, recognizes the theoretical advantages of the use of paper money. If the issuance of paper money could be limited to needs, it might be satisfactory. But, Pesch does not believe that in practice its issuance will be so limited. His arguments are: (1) a satisfactory criterion is lacking to determine how much money should be issued; (2) the printing presses can too easily be misused; (3) interest groups will pressure for an increased issue of money; (4) experience has shown that no paper money has for long remained of stable value. In general, "the gold standard is not perfect, but a paper standard is even less perfect" (V, 256). With Lexis, he holds that for the proper operation of a paper standard certain conditions are necessary which almost certainly will not be fulfilled: the public must be certain that even in times of financial embarrassment the state will not violate the limits of a suitable supply of money; and there must be no fear of wars, overspeculation, overextension of bank credit, or crises (V, 190). Paper money as a pure claim might be practical in a communistic society, but it is not practical for a free economy.

> In a communistic society where the central authority allots to each his work and his quantity of goods, perhaps a paper money without any value other than the fact that it is a mere order on the state's supply of goods will suffice. In a free economy, however, a good of generally recognized value is needed which can serve all other goods as a means of comparison. Otherwise exchange finds itself with completely in-

soluable difficulties, and loses all security and all confidence (V, 265–66).

With his customary flexibility Pesch admits that in certain extraordinary circumstances paper money may be the only practical means to cover an excessive need for money. But, he warns, the need must be beyond doubt; and he cautions that as soon as possible the nation must strive to regain its former metallic standard (V, 190).

2. The Value of Money

The value of money is a basic problem in monetary theory. Does money possess value? If so, what is the nature of this value? The more recent Anglo-American literature has paid relatively little attention to this aspect of monetary theory. Pesch here again demonstrates his predilection for fundamentals. Three categories of value are distinguished. The most important is the functional value of money which is its social exchange value as represented by its purchasing power. The most basic is the intrinsic value which makes it possible for money to perform its proper functions. The least important is the nominal value indicated by the state in terms of marks, dollars, schillings, etc. A divergence between these three species of value is possible (V, 194–98).

A subordinate, parallel question is whether money has utility. Pesch answers:

> Money acquires utility through its relation to other goods as the means for the circulation of these goods, for the sale of articles of need, etc., as a security for the satisfaction of future needs, "fide jussor futurae necessitatis" (St. Thomas). But the circumstance that the money is composed of a useful material constitutes ultimately the basis of the possibility for the use of money as a means of exchange. Thus it will be well to distin-

guish the utility proper to money as such from the other utility which the money has on account of its substance and its own material properties as gold or silver (V, 194, note 4).

While metallic money possesses all three types of value, paper money possesses only the nominal and functional. The latter ultimately depends on its property as legal tender and the confidence of the people (V, 187, 197).

Pesch's response to the nominalistic position as represented by Bendixen perhaps best brings out his views on the nature of the value of money. Bendixen claims that money in itself has no value, but merely represents the value of other goods. Pesch concedes that paper money in itself has no material value—paper money is the point in dispute—but claims that in exchange it does more than represent the value of all goods combined. It is also representative of a determinate, generally desired commodity with a relatively more constant value than most goods. The principle function of money is as a means of comparison of the value of other goods; and this function is best performed by money with an intrinsic value or by money connected with something possessing intrinsic value.

In reply to Bendixen's retort that the man is yet to be born who when viewing a country estate priced at 70,000 marks thinks of 50 pounds of gold, Pesch acknowledges that in ordinary affairs people do not think of the value of money in terms of gold. But when they think of a certain sum they do have a concept of a determinate value. That they have such a determinate concept and that this concept dominates exchange transactions comes ultimately to this that the money and the value of the money is connected with a precious metal. If this connection is wiped out, then for awhile people may still relate a "100 mark" certificate with a definite concept of value. But gradually this determinate concept will become more and more vague until finally the designation "100 marks" could just as well be arbitrarily replaced by a Kniesian

"100 hoho or sasa." The latter would be just as suitable to represent all possible goods as "100 marks" to which no longer the concept of a determinate value corresponds (V, 262–63).

The Bendixenian observation on gold (repeated rather frequently today) is that gold does not give value to money, but the value of gold is derived from the fact that it is used as money. Pesch calls this a confusion of price and value, of external and internal value. Legal statutes bestow on a definite quantity of a precious metal its coin name, designate the nominal value of the coin, the price of the money. But it is beyond the power of legal statutes to arbitrarily determine the intrinsic value of money; this depends on the same value determinants as are operative in the determination of the value of any other good.

A priori it is expected by Pesch that the same factors operative in the case of goods will be effective also in the determination of the value of money. In general, changes in the value of money may be due to changes in the substance value of the precious metal, or it may be in the functional value through changes in the demand or supply of money (V, 204). As in general value theory, utility and scarcity are the basic determinants of the value of money. However, the usefulness of money rests not on its application to the immediate satisfaction of wants, but on its characteristic as a means to acquire goods useful to satisfy wants. It is only in this sense that one can speak of the use value of money.

The individual use value of money depends on the individual, personal circumstances, the magnitude of the individual's wants and income. Pesch appeals to the teaching of the marginal utility theory (which he suspects is usually presented in too exact a fashion) that "the 'subjective' value of money is determined by one's income through the marginal utility of money, that is, by the last expenditure which with a given

income is still economically useful, thus by the satisfaction
of the last want which is covered" (V, 211). But it is the general
purchasing power of money, its social exchange value which
is the more important concept for the value of money. The
relation between the individual and social, the subjective and
objective aspects of the problem is clearly delineated in the
following synthesis:

> It is self-evident that monetary theory has to reckon also
> with the subjective valuation of money, which can vary much
> according to particular, individual circumstances. The indi-
> vidual income, the whole wealth pattern, influences the evalu-
> ation which is placed upon money in the private economy.
> Its buying power is measured by the height of the income.
> But the exchange still remains for the individual a social
> phenomenon which, with the social price pattern, confronts
> the individual as something objective. Not only is there an in-
> dividual, subjective buying power of money, but also a social,
> objective buying power which the individual must consider
> when reflecting on the distribution of his income according to
> his personal needs. Moreover, there is not merely a subjective
> measure of the value of money in and for the private economy.
> In social commerce there is an objective foundation for the
> determination of the value of money, based on its intrinsic
> value (V, 255–56).

The cost of production here, as in general value theory,
does not determine directly the value of the precious metal
and thus the value of money. Production costs operate indirectly through supply by limiting the profit on production.
For example, if costs rise above the mint rate of the monetary
metal, production will no longer be profitable. Nor can the
market price of the metal sink below the mint rate, for the
metal could be brought to the mint and converted into corresponding units of the money (V, 210).

In reference to the scarcity factor, special attention is paid to the quantity theory of money. Pesch may be classified as a moderate quantity theorist.

> The quantity theory, insofar as with moderation it makes the price level determined by the supply of money in circulation, is essentially correct. It would be impossible to explain satisfactorily the formation of prices without approaching the fundamental position of the quantity theory (V, 199).

He rejects any rigid form of the theory which would imply that a mathematically exact relationship can be established between the supply of money and the price level.

The supply factor is only one among various influences at work on the price level. The velocity of the circulation of money must also be considered. Nor is all money of the same quality. A considerable increase of "less valuable" money, for example, "depreciated banknotes," will have a particularly strong effect on the price level. Also the more general question of the demand and supply of goods must be analyzed.

Both direct and indirect effects of an increased supply of money take place. Directly, if the supply of money increases in proportion to the needs of the economy (the volume of trade) the value of money will decline, and the buying power of each monetary unit will decline. At the same time the introduction of the new money increases the demand in the market. The possessors of the new money come into the market with greater buying power. Another indirect influence is the lower interest rate due to the increased bank reserves because of the greater supply of money. The lower interest rate stimulates production, which increases the demand for labor, raw materials, etc. Thus the general price level rises, the buying power of money decreases (V, 213). Pesch could have added, however, that with an expanded production in time more products would flow into the market, which would have a tendency to lower prices.

In reference to the quantity theory's foreign trade sequence —high domestic prices leading to the export of money and thus lowering domestic prices—Pesch emphasizes that we are dealing with free, rational causes. Such a theory is too mechanical for him. And, he points out, in the case of paper money the excess money tends to stay in the home country. This free cause aspect was incorporated into the "currency theory" which Pesch would accept if this position is limited to inconvertible notes. Also, he would distinguish between financial issues, which are normally long-term, and mercantile issues, which usually are outstanding for a shorter period of time (V, 203–204).

With contemporary economists Pesch finds the problem of the measurement of the value of money difficult and yielding no completely satisfactory solution. It is a question here of the functional value of money. The most commonly accepted measure is a general price index. But, besides the practical problems involved in the construction of such a general index (a wholesale index is not accounted satisfactory), changes in the index do not indicate *per se* changes in the value of money. A decline in prices may be due to an improvement in the techniques of production or transportation and not to a rise in the intrinsic value of money. From a mere study of the price index "it cannot be satisfactorily established to what extent changes in the price level have their cause on the side of goods or on the monetary side" (V, 208).

Another possible measure of the value of money is the level of wages. But here, again, changes may be only a reflection of general economic conditions, improvements in industrial techniques or changes in the standard of living. In the particular case of a decline in the wholesale price of raw materials and semi-finished goods simultaneous with a more than negligible rise in wages a clear indication is offered that the rise in wages is due to a change in general economic conditions, and that the decline in the price of the product is not due to a change in the value of money. Otherwise with a declining price of his product the profit calculations of the entrepreneur would have caused him to seek to lower wages.

A third possible measure is the discount rate. But this primarily indicates the demand for capital and not the value of money in itself. It would be erroneous to claim that a high discount rate indicates a high value of money. Experience shows that periods of rising prices coincide with high discount rates.

In general, Pesch does not dispute the influence of changes in the value of money on prices, wages, and the discount rate; but he merely wishes to caution against an overemphasis and misinterpretation of this influence. Normally, the effects of monetary value changes operate indirectly through general causes, the totality of economic conditions—the changes in the cost of production and transportation, the cost of living, the income pattern of the community, increased demand for products, trade balances, and the balance of payments (V, 210).

3. The Goal of Monetary Policy

Stability in the value of money, to the extent it is practical, is the chief goal of Peschian monetary policy. In itself money is only a means to fulfill the end of the whole economic process, the providing for the needs of the people. Every monetary system which throws the economic system off-balance so that it is unable to achieve its primary task is a false system. While perfect stability is not to be hoped for, because of the very nature of money, still reasonable stability, eliminating violent decreases and increases in the value of money, is to be sought. "Every monetary system which places this stability in doubt

is incompatible with the demands of the common welfare"
(V, 206).

The explanation why perfect stability can never be attained
offers a penetrating response to the popular clamor for a
monetary standard with the same immutableness as found in
the measures of length and weight.

> The measure of material, *corporeal* objects can be exact and
> possess permanent validity. The measure of *value*, however,
> being concerned with *judgments of value*, unlike the measures
> of length and weight, offers no promise of complete exactness,
> but rather fluctuates undergoing a change if the foundation
> upon which it rests experiences a change. The value of money
> in itself is not an unconditional, stable magnitude as the units
> of our weight and extension systems. Furthermore the value
> of a good is indeed founded on its objective, physical condi-
> tions—the ability of the object to satisfy human wants, the
> difficulty or ease with which it can be acquired, i.e., the condi-
> tion of the supply—but in itself it is not something material
> or physical. Value is rather an estimation, and as such of its
> very nature involves a relation with the human mind. Thus
> the measure of value possesses different characteristics than
> the measures of length and weight (V, 134–35). (Italics in
> original.)

The numerous consequences of a depreciation in the value
of money are particularly deplored. Rational judgments about
price movements are impossible. Savings decline in value,
prompting savers to convert their money into real goods. The
security of loans dissolves. Speculation is encouraged. Production declines because of the insurmountable obstacles to
rational business decisions. Wage earners and persons of fixed
incomes are unjustly burdened. The state finds it difficult to
balance its budget, for costs are rising and income is uncertain.
And internationally the balance of prices between different

countries is disturbed and the countries with devalued currencies are unable to buy.

A practical question for monetary policy to solve is how to measure the monetary needs of the economy. The factors which must be weighed are: the sum of the products circulating in the market, the velocity of money, the quantity of money saved, the available substitutes for money (IV, 175–76).

CHAPTER SIX

DISTRIBUTION THEORY

MODERN theories of distribution are primarily studies of the exchange value of the factors of production. That the price paid for these production factors becomes the income of certain groups in the nation is a by-product of this analysis.[1] The classical economists, on the other hand, were primarily interested in the determination of the relative shares going to the different economic groups, specifically, the landowners, entrepreneurs, and laborers. These two approaches are necessarily closely linked together in a study of the modern capitalistic economy with its division of labor. But they are not identical; they are on different levels of analysis.[2] The modern per-unit approach is abstract, functional, concerned primarily with the economical distribution of resources. It seeks an

[1] Cf. Haley's comment: "Distribution theory continued to be limited in the main to analysis of the determinants of the *per unit rate* of remuneration of the factors of production. Although such analysis should contribute to an understanding of the determinants of the corresponding functional *shares* of the national income, little progress is to be reported with respect to this higher stage of distribution analysis" ("Value and Distribution," *op. cit.,* p. 26). (Italics in original.)

[2] See L. M. Fraser, *Economic Thought, op. cit.,* pp. 344–54, for a clear exposition of the contrast between the classical and the modern approaches.

identical principle determining all factor prices; and claims to possess such a principle from the side of demand in the principle of marginal productivity.[3] In that its conclusions are applicable to every type of economy it is wider in scope than the classical approach; but it is narrower than the latter, since its analysis is limited to the market-place. Also, it offers no or little guidance for economic welfare and policy, limiting itself to the positive aspect.[4]

The main problem posited by Pesch is essentially the classical economists' question: "On what does the magnitude of the individual income spheres depend?" (V, 554). Many of the later theoretical developments are incorporated into the answer, but fitted into a classical framework.

However, Pesch's analysis differs from that of the classical economists, since the distributive shares are not analyzed by a study of the forces of supply and demand alone. Or, it may be said, the forces of supply and demand are not permitted to operate mechanically. "There is no doubt that competition has an influence on the formation of income, but we cannot manage with 'supply and demand' alone, especially in the matter of wages" (V, 554). Nor does he accept unconditionally a solution via the marginal productivity analysis. For him, no solution is to be hoped for from a theory which starts from the supposed calculation of the individual contributions. Pro-

---

[3] As J. M. Clark has expressed it: "The marginal approach has the notable effect of making possible a homogeneous theory of distribution: at least on the demand side all shares are governed by an identical principle" ("Distribution," *Encyclopedia of the Social Sciences*, V [1937], p. 171; also in *Readings in the Theory of Income Distribution*, pp. 66–67).

[4] The modern approach is positive not necessarily in the sense that it states "what is," but rather it explains "what would be" if certain aberrations—such as unequal bargaining power, lack of complete knowledge, hindrances to freedom of entry, imperfect markets, kinked supply and demand curves—did not exist. And to the extent that the removal of these diverging influences would bring about the ideal "what is," this approach may be said to offer a certain guidance for economic welfare and policy.

duction is due to a heterogeneous cause. In a marginal productivity analysis of such a production "one operates only with 'unknowns' if it is desired to make the particular causality of each one of the factors in reference to the return from the production (the value of the consumer goods [Böhm-Bawerk] or the product [v. Wieser]) the starting point of a not imaginary reckoning" (V, 555).

The starting point for Pesch is that all who cooperate in the production of goods contribute their personal or material performance. The distribution problem becomes a question of reimbursement for this personal or material performance. The question which thus emerges is: "According to which principle must this reimbursement take place in order to be recognized as economically correct?" (V, 557).

The ultimate principle in distribution, as in every phase of the economic process, can be no other than the principle ruling and regulating the whole economic process: the goal of the economy, the providing for the needs of the people, conformable to the then attained cultural standards. Other points of view, or goals, which must be coordinated with this ruling principle are: the persons contributing their material and personal performance for economically useful production must find the recompense due them; and the development of the productive resources and facilities of the nation must be safeguarded and provided for. "All these points of view of justice and economic wisdom come into consideration for the theory of income formation" (V, 558).

Lest this emphasis on the principle of satisfying needs be misinterpreted as a denial of the profit motive, Pesch explicitly states its necessity, as a motive in economic actions:

> If the principle of satisfying needs replaces the principle of unlimited gain, thus not in the least is the striving for gain thereby excluded as a *motive;* however it no longer constitutes

the highest *norm*, but must be subordinated to the requirements of the national economic task *(ibid.)*.[5]

Here distribution is not treated as a mere private economic
problem, but is considered from the national aspect. For
example, wages are no longer a mere cost, but also the source
of income for a highly important group in the nation. The
accumulation of wealth is not only for the enrichment of the
entrepreneur, but is also a necessary means for the continua-
tion and perfection of the nation's productive equipment.

A sharp distinction between production costs and productive services runs through this entire analysis. In a money
economy production costs are the monetary costs of production, the amount the entrepreneur must pay out to produce—
his payments for raw materials, wages, the use of machines.
Productive services are the performance of the field's fruitfulness, of the productivity of the means of production worked
by men, of human labor power's own productivity.

> These services, these personal and material performances,
> determine the income of each one: the landowner receives the
> rent; the laborer, wages; the owner of the means of production
> in the widest sense, a corresponding reward for the applica-
> tion of these means of production to the production process
> (V, 693).

In the Peschian system four sources of income are distinguished: the rent for land, interest, wages, and the entrepreneurial profit. Each of these will be treated in some detail in
the remaining sections of this chapter.

---

[5] Harris by a mistranslation of the German word *"keineswegs"* gives an incorrect impression of the place of the profit motive in the Peschian system. He
translates the pertinent words of this sentence thus: "Still it does *not* follow
that when the principle of satisfying needs supersedes the principle of unlimited striving for gain the motive of private gain will *necessarily* be excluded" *(op. cit.,* p. 46). (Italics added.) There is a great deal of difference
between the meaning of the terms "not necessarily" and "not in the least."
See page 144 for another example where Pesch says that a striving for gain,
which is moderate, is necessary for the national welfare.

1. Wages

"Labor is not a commodity" but a personal action sums up Heinrich Pesch's concept of labor and his approach to the problem of wage determination (V, 563). To understand his treatment of the subject it must be borne in mind also that the wage contract is a *contractus sui generis,* that the worker is a producer not a mere means of production, and that the ultimate goal of work is not goods, but the well-being of all the participants and of society. One conclusion drawn from this humanistic concept of labor is that the identically same "laws" do not underlie the formation of the price of goods and the wage of labor (V, 631).

Pesch rejects the view that the wage question can be adequately solved by the arbitrariness or avarice of either the employer or employee, or the power relation existing between organizations of these two groups. The matter will be satisfactorily solved only if principles are adhered to which will satisfy the requirements of the true general welfare. This means that the purpose of the economy and the demands of justice must be considered. Thus in his exposition Pesch refers to two principles: the covering of needs and equivalence. In practice the principle of equivalence is considered sufficient. The covering-of-needs principle as a determinant of the wage is based on the social philosophic foundation that labor of every type is a good of man derived from nature to enable him to work, and is a conclusion derived from the goal of the economy that the purpose of economic activity is to provide for the needs of the people. Including all economic activities, but with an emphasis on labor, Pesch develops this thought:

> The immediate end, to which economic activity according to its nature is directed, the end, to which the laboring man with

the same natural and ethical necessity strives, by which he cares for, and has the duty to care for, the support of his life and the lives of those of his family, and which he himself with right seeks to attain, and by which he strives to better his lot, this end is in practice normally, above all, the providing for his needs, the securing and improving his welfare. . . . This right and this duty of working, this natural, immediate goal of labor remains valid within the society, and here must find its recognition, protection and realization. . . .

Since, however, the working man labors within society, since the product of his labor is destined for the satisfaction of the wants of another—he may work for a definite customer or for the market—the labor takes on in addition a social character; it has also a social goal, is therefore, as said, burdened with social duties. Too, society cannot remain indifferent whether and in which way the satisfaction of the wants of its members is provided for, whether and in which way the natural goal of social living-together and working-together finds its fulfillment (I, 38).

Here we find developed the dual thought that as an individual man receives from nature the right and ability, and also the concomitant duty, to support himself, to earn his livelihood; and that as a member of society, his work in conjunction with that of others is to support all the members of society, including himself. Therefore, unless it is denied that nature has provided men with the ability to fulfill their obligation to support themselves and their family—the individual argument—and that the goal of the economy is to provide for the needs of all the people, it must be held that in modern circumstances labor power is of sufficient value to enable them to earn a family living wage. For, in the modern, division-of-labor economy the common and only source of revenue for the great majority of men is their wage.

This minimum, derived from the individual purpose of work and the more general goal of the economy, is an absolute minimum applicable to all types of work, normal conditions supposed. A relative minimum, on the other hand, is "the lowest, still just, wage for a definite type and performance (time or piece) of labor in a definite business" (V, 630).[6] The absolute minimum corresponds to the necessary character of labor; the relative refers to the free character. The former under normal circumstances is something that a laborer cannot forego, since it is required for his livelihood. Greater freedom may be exercised in the determination of the relative minimum, for it presupposes the absolute.

The absolute minimum is not to be confused with an "existence" minimum; it rather posits a "convenient" standard of living. This is a standard worthy of a man's dignity in keeping with the circumstances of the given time and place. The proximate determinant of the content of this standard of living is the "general standard of culture and consequently the public opinion varying according to time and place" (V, 632). Unless provided for by other sources (e.g., social security or a welfare fund), the minimum must be sufficient to cover sickness and old-age expenses. Moreover, it is not reckoned on an individual basis, but is to provide for a normal family. Thus, Pesch's absolute minimum may be characterized as a family, cultural, living wage (V, 631–32, 635–39).

[6] Through an unfortunate error Harris defines Pesch's *absolute* minimum by presenting the definition of the *relative* minimum: and also within this misapplied definition through a mistranslation of the German word "gerechte" the absolute minimum is made to appear as a "legal" rather than a "just" rate. The pertinent passage in Mr. Harris' article reads as follows: ". . . Pesch proposes the establishment of an absolute minimum as 'the lowest legal rate for a definite kind and performance of labor in a given business' (V, 630). These minimum rates are to serve as a floor for relative wages. The former are to be fixed by the state, while the latter are to be settled by bargaining between associations of employers and employees" (*op. cit.,* p. 46.) The role of the state in Pesch is discussed on page 136. Perhaps it is sufficient to say now that the wages discussed here, and incorrectly called absolute, are not to be fixed by the state. Even the absolute minimum as defined by Pesch is not considered to be fixed by the state; at least there is nothing in the original of the passage quoted that states this.

Nor is this "living wage" theory to be confused with the classical "cost of production" or "necessary" wage theories. These classical theories took the genetic approach, inquiring what is required to produce the laborers. The "living wage" theory adopts the teleological approach, asking what is the purpose of labor. It is true that in the "cost of production" theories a certain teleological aspect is contained; however it is not so much that man is the goal, but production and its continuance. Also in its extreme form production wage theories lead to a bare existence minimum; while the "living wage" posits, as seen above, a cultural minimum. Too, the latter is a minimum *juris* which even for the hope of greater profits the entrepreneur may not violate; the classical theories were a minimum *facti,* below which the short-run competitive or a power position could lower the "competitive" price of labor (V, 627–28).

Pesch's second fundamental principle for the determination of the wage is the principle of equivalence. The wage contract, even though a *contractus sui generis,* is still a contract, and thus subject to the requirement of justice that an equivalent return must be paid for what is received. From this emerges the important question: according to which point of view is the equality of value between the work and the wage to be determined? Here Pesch introduces a distinction which at first sight may seem subtle, but which is of importance for a proper understanding of his wage norm. "The wage does not pay for the work in the *passive* sense, i.e., the effect, the product of the labor. . . . The wage pays for the labor in the *active* sense, the working of the laborer" (V, 642–43). (Italics in original.)

> It is well to observe that the wage as the return for the value of the labor is not a return for the fruit, the product of the labor, but is a return only for the labor considered in itself;

it is not an equivalence for the product brought forth by the labor—this falls to the property of the entrepreneur—but is an equivalence for the working of the labor in its particular kind, magnitude, circumstances (V, 629).

The product, however, is not without influence on the determination of the value of the labor. First of all, the type of product determines the type of work. And the wage must be a complete compensation "for everything which the laborer brings and offers, applies and sacrifices to this; thus for the working of a labor-power proportional to the desired work during a definite time; and with consideration for all the special sacrifices, which from the nature of the thing are bound up with this type of work" (V, 644).

Also, the value of the product indirectly determines the wage, since the effective demand for the product leads to an effective demand for the labor. "If the labor performance possesses no use-value (for the entrepreneur) corresponding to the wage, then also the supposit of an effective demand for such labor is lacking," which means that the labor has been employed in a production not corresponding to a want of the consumers. In fact, from the intimate relation between labor performances and product value, Pesch concludes that in practice it is not necessary to speak of a twofold principle, the covering of needs and equivalence, in wage determination. "Equivalence remains rather the self-evident requirement for the practical application of the principle of providing for needs" (V, 629).

The assumption on which this simplification is based is that normal conditions prevail in the economy. On the part of the laborer are assumed normal ability, normal performance, and normal wants. On the side of the entrepreneur the assumptions are a general economic environment sufficiently favorable to enable him to pay at least the absolute minimum wage, the production of a product for which there is a sufficient demand, and normal efficient shop conditions (V, 630–31, 643–44).[7]

Pesch's recognition of the influence of the product and its value on the determination of the wage is not to be interpreted as if he accepts unconditionally the productivity theory in general, or the marginal productivity theory in particular. On the productivity of labor depends the *possibility* of paying the wage; it determines the upper-limit of the wage level.[8] But increased productivity offers the laborer "only the *possibility* of a better lot, actually it in no wise secures for him a high or even suitable wage" (V, 606). Pesch observes that women, whose labor performance is equal to that of men, do not always receive the same wage as men. If the normal conditions assumed by Pesch are realized then there should be no disharmony between productivity, the value of the labor performance, and the requirements for a suitable standard of living.

Prescinding from his general criticism of the marginal productivity analysis, particularly the doubt of its applicability to a production founded on a heterogeneous causality, Pesch looks with favor on the marginalist's treatment of wage theory as a logical consequence of general value theory. His approbation, however, is qualified to this extent: "Only the subjec-

[7] Perhaps Harris oversimplifies the Peschian system, when he states unconditionally: "It is then, not merely the principle of needs, but also productivity which Pesch holds to be the basis for determining 'relative wages'" (*op. cit.*, p. 46). Harris is correct when he quotes Pesch's isolated statement in Volume III, where he combines productivity and standard of living apparently on the same level. But, in view of the full explanation in Volume V, it is clear that this is to be understood as an indirect influence only. The two norms will be satisfied if ideal conditions prevail. It seems that Harris has misunderstood the value of labor or equivalence principle in the passive sense rather than the active.

[8] See Oswald v. Nell-Breuning, "Lohn, Lohngerechtigkeit," *Wörterbuch der Politik,* III: *Zur Sozialen Frage* (1949), col. 147.

tive evaluation of the entrepreneur is not to determine the value of the work" (V, 608). If the Peschian position were formulated in marginal-productivity terms, it would be that a satisfactory means must be found to raise the marginal productivity of the workers, and to guarantee that they are paid their full marginal product.[9] The latter aim has reference to the static condition, while the former aim has a dynamic reference. For, a higher wage-level is desired because "well-paid laborers work better than those poorly paid" and a rise in wages increases the purchasing power of the mass of workers, which "protects domestic production from crises, expands and solidifies the market which lies nearest the domestic producer and offers him less competition" than found in foreign markets (III, 185).

From the preceding discussion the aims of the Peschian wage policy may be easily summarized. The general goal is the satisfaction of the needs of the people; the particular, a rising wage level satisfying the principles of need and equivalence. To achieve this, an equitable bargaining relationship

---

[9] Once we leave the rigid assumptions of perfect competition, or even pure competition, there are various possibilities whereby real wages may be raised without a decrease of employment. With pure competition, the marginal productivity of the workers may be raised by the application of more capital in relation to the labor supply, increased efficiency of the workers, or increased demand for the product. In the context of uncertainty attached to profit expectation Fellner explains how a change in real wages may affect the level of unemployment. (See *Competition Among the Few, op. cit.,* pp. 266–72.) In a discussion of oligopoly under conditions of cyclical change, L. G. Reynolds argues that employment (and output) are not directly affected by changes in the cost-price relations, because of the shape of cost and revenue functions. (See "Relations Between Wage Rates, Costs and Prices," *American Economic Review,* XXXII, Supplement [March, 1942], pp. 276–81; also in *Readings in the Theory of Income Distribution,* pp. 296–302.) Besides cases of deliberate exploitation, G. F. Bloom presents cases of non-deliberate exploitation due to such causes as a less than perfectly elastic labor supply curve or rigid prices. (See "A Reconsideration of the Theory of Exploitation," *Quarterly Journal of Economics,* LV [May, 1941], pp. 419–33; also in *Readings in the Theory of Income Distribution,* pp. 251–68.)

must be restored. The chief instrument to restore equitable bargaining relationships is collective bargaining, which is the central notion of the Peschian policy program.

It does not follow, however, that because collective bargaining is the chief instrument of policy, this theory may be called a "bargaining" or "force" theory of wages.[10] First of all, collective bargaining is not necessarily a question of power relationships, at least, no more so, than in the case of an employer bargaining with an individual employee. Pesch explicitly rejects a solution of the wage question by power relationships. Secondly, he denies that from a relationship of power any principles can arise for theory. Of one who holds the contrary, he asks whether "this is a question of fashioning a theory" (V, 608).

Because collective bargaining is such an important element in the Peschian wage policy, a more complete consideration must be given to a study of its nature, advantages, and defects. It is defined as "a collective agreement between one or more entrepreneurs or employers' organization on the one side, and a labor organization on the other, with the aim and effect of

---

[10] In an unrestrained criticism Harris has charged: "For all the ethical verbiage in which his ideas concerning wages are couched, what Pesch really gives is a 'force' theory of wages, which, incidentally, is to a great extent exemplified in present practices of trade-unions. If the impersonal determination of rewards by the market is generally superseded by 'bargaining power,' as Pesch seems to propose, the determination of wages and other income shares would degenerate into a contest of organized grab." (*Op. cit.*, pp. 46–47.) From the discussion above, it should be clear that Pesch has introduced collective bargaining only as a means of implementing policy, and definitely rejects it as a "theory" of wages. The weaknesses of wage determination in markets other than perfect or pure are not corrected by calling such wage determination "the impersonal determination of rewards by the market." If perfect, or at least, pure competition conditions prevail, Pesch, too, should have no objection against such an "impersonal" determination. However, for the reasons mentioned in the text, pages 133 and 134 below, he believes that such ideal conditions are not normally to be expected in the determination of wages. In general, it may be said it is unscientific to compare the ideal of one system with another stripped of such a protective covering. Pesch, too, is aware of the many problems involved in collective bargaining, see pages 134–136 below.

establishing binding determinants (regularly considered as minimum norms) for the content of future individual contracts of labor, and in addition also for the general regulating of conditions of labor, the relations between entrepreneurs and laborers" (III, 158). This definition is not claimed to be theoretically perfect; it is offered rather as a description of the agreements found in Germany at the time. A major difference from collective bargaining as known in the United States will be noted, in that the above description is more applicable to the notion of a "master contract." It is not the actual job contract, nor a detailed blueprint, according to which future contracts are settled; it is more of a directive for eventual labor agreements. (Also, in Germany adherence could be legally enforced.) In it general norms are to be agreed upon which will determine the content of the individual contracts to be made in the future. Its main objective is to offer the essential content for the individual agreements (III, 159–64).

Collective bargaining is approved because it is "one of the most effective means offered in contemporary history to better immediately and most extensively the living conditions of the dependent workers, to assert their proper interest *vis-à-vis* the owner of capital, and indeed, for the advantage of the whole national economy" (III, 185). In particular it is a means to raise the wages and shorten the hours of work, whenever practically possible.

In the context of freedom, collective bargaining is required to protect the freedom of the workers. And this is important, for "a development of the economy such as we have witnessed would be unthinkable without free laborers" (III, 173). Pesch denies that this advantage of freedom is completely found in the individualistic idea of freedom. He opposes the individualistic system with its "legal" equality which destroys freedom in reality and means the capitulation of the laborer to the employer. "The latter could wait for his money, the laborer could not wait for his livelihood" (*ibid.*). But, though the employer does not need the individual laborer, he does need labor-power. And the laborers organize to utilize this need, to equalize the weapons in the battle to determine labor relations. Thus, "the principle of collective bargaining in its complete application signifies the introduction of a truly 'free' and 'equality-of-rights' labor contract" (III, 174). In the background of this development is the idea that an unreasonable and harmful competition among the laborers themselves is a possibility. This may be due not only to the profit motive, but may be made excessive through need. It is the task of collective bargaining to give the workers protection from such unreasonable competition.

Also, the order created in labor relations by collective bargaining is to the advantage of the employer. In general these are two: (1) an elimination of undesirable competition by rivals who may seek to lower wages in order to cut prices; (2) the establishment of peace and order within the business. It is not expected that collective bargaining will eliminate every disturbance in industrial relations. But is peace to be sought "at any price"?

The many difficulties which have been urged against collective bargaining are not ignored by Pesch. Briefly, the main objections and his comments are:

(1) Collective bargaining only substitutes the tyranny of the union for that of the entrepreneur. However, every community or organization requires a sacrifice from its members —this is true even of the natural societies, the family and the state. The tyranny which is often found is due to human defects, which indeed deserves censure, but which can be overcome; it is not a necessary property of an institution sound in itself (III, 178).

(2) Collective bargaining leads to a demoralizing equality,

represents a leveling downwards, favoring the ungifted, the lazy, the weak. But, in modern mass production methods a certain leveling downwards is already found, and the job standards used are not perfect. It is believed that collective bargaining can perfect job standards superior to those common in individual contract evaluations. Signs of this superiority are to be found in the requirements of the minimum performance for the minimum wage. Also, it is not forbidden to the individual laborer by personal industry and superior work to acquire a better wage. And, where piecework schedules are used, this leveling-down charge loses much of its force. Again, special trained officials of the industry can make better estimates of the peculiarities of each individual plant and job. A more serious danger than the one alleged, in the mind of Pesch, is that the less gifted and weak will be laid off if business declines, since collective bargaining by limiting the entrepreneur's freedom to lower wages will tend to a reduction of the number employed (V, 179).

(3) Entrepreneurs fear that the union will mix itself in the affairs of the business; that freedom of disposition of employees will no longer be theirs; that the necessary adaptability to changing business conditions will be restricted. Part of this fear is due to lack of experience with collective bargaining. Still these problems must be given consideration in the future collective contracts. Absolute perfection in these questions will not be attained. "One may be satisfied, if in a just examination without prejudice, the advantages of collective bargaining—everything considered—are greater than the apparent or real disadvantages" (III, 180).

(4) Unsolved are a whole series of juridical questions, and legislative problems. The number and magnitude of these difficulties, according to Pesch, must not be minimized; but he believes that good will and reason can solve them.

Pesch's conclusion of his study of collective bargaining is

that the development is not completed; there are difficulties, but no impossibilities (III,184).

What is the legitimate activity of the state in wage policy? In view of the general social principle that political regulation is permissible only when no other effective regulation is possible and the public welfare unconditionally requires it, it is held that if these conditions are fulfilled the state may set up general legal forms and juridical processes necessary to realize the wage norms. It may, to the extent required, protect the rights and enforce the duties flowing from the collective agreements; for it would be unworthy of the state if such matters should be a mere question of the relative power of the parties. But, management and labor make their own contracts; they themselves determine its content.

> But the concluding and content of the contract itself, however, is and remains above all a matter of the parties. Here the law can determine only the extrinsic limits of what is legally permissible. And insofar as the social factors prove themselves capable of the social regulation of the entire collective bargaining, the autonomy required for capable development should be left to them. Political compulsion in all these matters is not the first, but the last thing (III, 189–90).

Pesch rejects any consideration of the state determining all wages (V, 655). Even a legal absolute minimum wage— which most of his followers would favor today—is not a clear-cut case. He presents the practical economic difficulties a legal minimum involves, and then admits that the weight of the arguments may be viewed differently by various authors.

2. Profits

In the question of profits the only agreement among economists seems to be that it is the most controversial topic in the theory of distribution. As Fraser has aptly expressed it, "the theory of profit is by common consent the most recalcitrant element in the whole structure of value and distribution analysis." [11] Of the various divisions presented of modern theories, Professor Gordon's has met with some general acceptance, and may prove useful here as a frame of reference.[12] He divides profit theories into three groups, based on whether profits are considered (1) as a long-run determinate return for the exercise of a productive function—with a host of concepts to explain what this function is; or, (2) as a final residual after interest on capital and wages of management—the "pure" profit or residual approach; or, (3) as "unearned" income, being a result of institutional monopolies.

The Peschian profit theory is in the main functional, stressing the organizing, directing, and risk-bearing activities of the entrepreneur. His method is not to define profits and then to identify their income recipient. His treatment is rather a study of the income of the entrepreneur.[13] This entrepreneurial income is conceived as an autonomous income, like wages, rent, and interest. And though attributable to various causes, it is considered as a unified whole. Pesch opposes any actual (in opposition to a mental, attributable) division of the entrepreneur's income into the three elements of a wage for the work of directing, a gain of capital for the normal return of

[11] Fraser, *Economic Thought, op. cit.*, p. 213. Cf. also the statement of Fellner and Haley, "The theory of profit and rent contains many controversial issues." ("Introduction," to *Readings in the Theory of Income Distribution*, p. x.)

[12] R. A. Gordon, "Enterprise, Profits, and the Modern Corporation," *Explorations in Economics, op. cit.*, pp. 307–11; also in *Readings in the Theory of Income Distribution*, pp. 560–65.

[13] To avoid repetition the question, "Who is the entrepreneur?" will be discussed below, particularly in reference to the modern corporation, pages 141–143. Here it may be useful to note that Pesch calls an "entrepreneur" those "independent producers and traders who at their own risk organize and direct the production, financing, and displaying of economic goods in order to obtain a gain from the difference between the cost of production and the price obtained by the sale of the product and commodities" (V, 691).

capital plus a risk-premium, and a residual called the "entrepreneurial profit." He believes that any actual division along these lines leads to an overemphasis of this income as an unearned gain from capital. This is particularly true, if the return on borrowed money and the return on the money the entrepreneur invests in his own business is confused. Too, it would be a limited view to consider this income as if it were a labor income, unless the term is used in its widest sense, and the labor is recognized as one but not the sole source (V, 665–67, 672, 685).[14]

In this matter two questions must be distinguished: whence this income rises, and the reason why it is paid to the entrepreneur.[15] This gain is derived immediately from the sale of the product, mediately from the production. It is the surplus of the gross return over the production cost, or the difference between what is received for the sale of the product and what is paid out for the production. Concerning this there is no dispute.

The controversial problem is what justifies the entrepreneur to claim this surplus, what activity or contribution justifies his claim. Again, there is no controversy that in the juridical order the formal foundation of this claim is the property right of the entrepreneur in the product. This follows from the essence of the modern wage contract. The materials and labor service belong to the entrepreneur; thus the product and the return from the sale of it, also, belong to him.

The more important, intrinsic justification of the claim of

14 Jean Marchal's most recent exposition of the theory of profits adopts this same "global analysis" in contrast to the modern "atomistic analysis" ("The Construction of a New Theory of Profit," *American Economic Review*, XLI [September, 1951], pp. 549–65). In the later stages of his theory Marchal goes beyond the Peschian profit theory. However, the new elements introduced can be found in Pesch's analysis of the market.

15 As Gordon has expressed it: "It is important to bear in mind, however, that accounting for the *origin* and *existence* of an income does not in itself explain its *allocation* to particular persons or classes" (*op. cit.*, p. 315). (Italics in original.)

the entrepreneur is based on his personal and material performance. His personal function is both passive and active. His
passive contribution is that he bears the risk of the enterprise.
This includes the technical risk, e.g., failures in the process
of production, and the economic risk, possible failure to find
a profitable sale for the product (III, 89). "He, who bears the
danger, has now also a claim to the gain. . . . The greater
the risk the greater the gain" (V, 691). His active function is
to organize and direct the business. This includes all the
activities necessary to set the enterprise in operation and to
continue it in operation—the bringing together and keeping
available all the elements of production and of selling, "the
correlation of all the elements and factors" required for the
success of the business (III, 89).

Pesch is fully aware that the modern rise of capitalism and
mass production has widened the scope of entrepreneurial
activities.

> He (the entrepreneur) will observe the market seeking to in-
> fluence it, in practice making it serve the profit interest of the
> enterprise. It is a question here of the important identification
> of the demand, of the possibility of reimbursement, of the
> profitability. Latent wants, gaps in the providing for needs
> are to be spurred on; new wants aroused; competition elimi-
> nated; means of influencing the masses, of mass suggestion are
> to be applied. Thereby the calculation, the reckoning of costs
> and prices are made more difficult (III, 90).[16]

[16] It is difficult to understand Harris' gratuitous charge: "Pesch's inability
to see the difference in the idea of gain as it applies to modern and to medieval
conditions, respectively, is responsible for his erroneous or meaningless conclusions respecting risk and profit, on the one hand, and interest and the formation of capital, on the other. But at the bottom of it all is the fact that his
outlook upon modern economic life was strongly controlled by habits of
thought associated with handicraft industry and petty trade" (*op. cit.*, p. 49).
If further evidence, in addition to the exposition given in the text, is desired
of the correct view of Pesch on modern economic life, see his treatment of
enterprise, Vol. III, pp. 37–341.

These activities make a high degree of demand on the initiative of the entrepreneur.

The material performance or contribution of the entrepreneur is founded on the investment in the enterprise of his capital-goods, which are necessary conditions and instrumental causes of the production. The value of the yield from the machines, land, factories must receive a return to be included in the sales price; and this is in addition to the costs of those things used up in the production, the materials, the depreciation of the machines, etc. That these yields as such have a special value is clearly seen from the fact that these instruments of production may be profitably rented out.

> Thus, it is clear how the "interest on capital" (called "original," also "natural interest") constitutes a *part* of the entrepreneur's profit as a recompense for the material performance of the entrepreneur, for the yield of the conditions and instrumental causes, which make the production possible, and increase the productivity of the worker (V, 692).[17]

Though Pesch thus recognizes interest on capital invested as one of the contributing sources of the entrepreneur's income, he does not accept unequivocally any of the prevailing capital interest theories. He admits that rightly they have emphasized that produced instruments of capital are fruitful aids to human labor; that they greatly increase productivity; and that in a social order founded on private property they constitute a source of the entrepreneurial income. But, taken alone, they are unable adequately to explain why a surplus value exists. For example, in reference to Böhm-Bawerk's celebrated agio- or time-differential theory of the roundaboutness of production, Pesch comments: "Thus in any case the so-called 'value-productivity' of capital still requires an essential

[17] It will be recalled that this part attributable to the interest on capital is only a mental division, since the entrepreneurial income is considered as a unified whole.

supplement by the special activity of the entrepreneur, if a loss instead of a gain should not be the end of the tune" (V, 671). Buyers must be found, if the production of capital goods is to have economic value.

But is Pesch's functional theory of "profits" in conformity with modern economic data? How can the personal entrepreneurial functions be attributed to the modern stockholder who apparently performs no active service in the enterprise?

Pesch is fully aware of the division between ownership and the actual directing so common in the modern corporation. He explains in detail how the officials of the modern corporation, who often are not the owners, assume the actual directing of the enterprise. Nevertheless, his position is that the owner remains the entrepreneur, for he is the bearer of the legal rights and responsibilities. From this legal point of view

> . . . even the highest "official" remains only an officer entrusted with the functions of directing; in the legal sense he is not the entrepreneur. The bearer of the rights in the enterprise, and in this sense the entrepreneur, is only the owner of the enterprise. Again, as owner of the enterprise is to be considered anyone in whose name the business is carried on and for whose profit and risk the business is developed. It is not necessary that the owner of the enterprise be personally active in the business; he can leave the guidance of his business to his officers and employees without ceasing thereby to be considered legitimately as the owner of the enterprise and in this sense as the entrepreneur (III, 100).

Even when the director performs the entrepreneurial functions of directing, "it is the concern of the entrepreneur (the stockholders) to find suitable personnel for this and to combine them" (V, 691, note). Nor does the fact that the small stockholders are passive in this regard, since they lack effective voice in the corporation, take away from the stockholders as a group this responsibility and right. Perhaps one may call this partial form of entrepreneurship an incomplete type; and the person who invests his own capital and directs his own business a full or complete entrepreneur (III, 97).

Professor Gordon recommends that the entrepreneurial function be most properly regarded as the active and dynamic leadership in the business, whether or not we may wish to call the return for this function by the conventional term "profit." [18] In the modern large corporation these functions would be performed by the executives who exercise "control" though their ownership be small or negligible. The difference between this and the Peschian position is partly terminological, and partly a question of posing different problems. There is no disagreement about the fact that there is often a division of ownership from control in the modern large corporation. Terminologically, the issue is whether to label the owner or the managing executive the "entrepreneur." The etymological approach would favor the executive; the legal approach, the owner. In the modern corporation the responsibility for the firm's existence rests ultimately with the owner—at least, in the sense, that if dissatisfied, even the small stockholder can sever his relations with the particular enterprise. But the basic difference between the two positions is that two distinct, though related, problems are discussed. Gordon inquires first of all about the entrepreneurial function of control; the income received for this is secondary in the discussion. Pesch studies the question of the sources of the owner's income; the function of control is only one of these sources.

Perhaps the modern picture has become blurred, because a certain group have arrogated to themselves powers that rightly belong to others. Or, is the difficulty that certain owners, who are not performing the full traditional function of the entrepreneur, are still claiming a reward for work they

18 Gordon, *op. cit.*, p. 314.

have left undone? If so, this is a problem that a wise economic policy should correct.

However this may be in the case of the modern large corporation, upon what does the amount of profit of any enterprise depend? In the first instance, it depends on the size of the surplus of selling price over production and selling costs. And this surplus in turn depends on the technical and economic efficiency of the whole business, "on the appropriate organization of production and sales, the correct measurement of admissible costs, on the adaptation of the quantity and quality of the product to the need, then also on the actual power position of the enterprise in the market (monopoly, etc.)" (V, 694–95).

On the assumption that the owner has not only invested some capital in the enterprise but also performs the personal entrepreneurial functions, when is the return adequate? From the causal point of view the profit is adequate, if it corresponds to the material and personal performance of the entrepreneur, providing him with an interest for his capital invested, a wage for his entrepreneurial labor, a reward for undertaking the risk. Or, teleologically, it can be said that a profit is adequate if it fulfills the ends which it should serve. On the same assumption that the owner makes both a material and personal contribution, what are the ends which the profit is supposed to serve? [19]

(1) It should secure for the entrepreneur a livelihood in keeping with his station in life. Indeed, perhaps even a big

---

[19] Because he has overlooked this assumption is probably one of the reasons why Harris states: "The fact that profits involve much that is sheer gamble and, given effective competition, tend on the whole to disappear, would seem to preclude the possibility of establishing any relationship between them and 'need' " (*op. cit.*, p. 50). His fundamental error is that he is attempting to apply Knight's concept of "pure" profit to Pesch's profit norms based on a functional concept of profit. Thus, all that he has succeeded in doing here— as elsewhere—is to prove that Pesch is not a follower of Knight.

gain still will appear too small to luxuriously living entrepreneurs, if it is not so extensive as to cover their luxury
expenditures. But such claims are not norms for the concept
of a livelihood in keeping with one's station in life.

(2) The gain should offer sufficient incentive for the con-
tinuation and improvement of the business. This remains
within the bounds of an entirely justified striving for gain (V,
695).

Lest anyone suspect Pesch only tolerates the striving for
gain, because of his insistence on the higher principle of providing for the needs of the people, and would seek to eliminate
it in the "ideal" order, it may be well to quote his added
encomium of profits—why they are required for the national
welfare.

Striving for gain, regulated and kept within bounds by
ethical norms, is not only justified in itself, but is also *necessary for the welfare of the nation.* The providing for the needs
of all the people can only be something advantageous and
progressively satisfying through a suitable capital formation.
Every sound progressive development of the national economic process presupposes the presence of wealth, even great
wealth. The means for the formation of wealth, however, is
income. And thus, also a favorable income formation lies in
the interest of national progress (*ibid.*).[20] (Italics in original.)

The minimum gain which will satisfy the entrepreneur is
the return which money loans are receiving. Otherwise there
is wanting a sufficient motive to undertake the entrepreneurial
responsibilities and activities. It is not so easy to determine

---

[20] This quotation alone should be sufficient to reveal the inaccuracy of
Harris' statement: "The doctrine (Pesch's) may accordingly be restated as
follows: Prices and distributive shares are 'just' when the rewards to the
economic agents or the costs of their continued performance, due allowance
being made for reserves, are neither more nor less than what is required to
furnish the agents with a livelihood commensurate with their station in society
(mit dem standesgemässes Lebensunterhalt)." (*Op. cit.,* p. 45.)

the maximum he should receive. But an indirect criterion may be used by examining the source of the gain. "The profit may not be derived from excessive prices, nor be attributable to exploitation of the consumer and laborer" (V, 696).

The tendency of the entrepreneurial incomes toward an equality is admitted by Pesch with some qualification. Given perfect or even pure competition entrepreneurs will seek that field where the greatest gain is hoped for; and thus prices will tend to decline and/or costs through competition for the factors of production will rise, either or both of which will cause profits to decline. But, Pesch believes, freedom of movement is not always a realistic assumption. A shift of present capital investments may not be possible at all or only with considerable financial loss; or entrepreneurs may lack the education and training required in the industry where more lucrative returns are being realized.

In the modern economy "the public welfare of the nation appears to be essentially dependent on the successful activity of private entrepreneurs" (III, 96). And "where all business initiative flags and fails," successful business enterprises so important for the national welfare will not be found (*ibid.*).

3. Rent

"The theory of rent has played a very small part indeed in recent theoretical discussions." [21] Thus Professor Haley sums up the dormant status of rent theory during the past decade and a half. However, there has been one important development— though its origin antedates the twentieth century—namely, the tendency to depart from the traditional identification of rent as a payment to a particular factor of production, land; and to call "rent" any surplus return to a factor of production

[21] Haley, *op. cit.,* p. 45.

because of a preferential position.[22] But, it should be noted that this identification is concerned with the concept "relative" rent, and in itself says nothing about "absolute" rent. The question whether the latter is a separate income category depends on the issue whether land should be identified with capital. Should no distinction of importance for economic theory exist, then at least for the sake of simplification, it would be better to group land and capital within the same category.

Pesch, too, extended the concept of "relative" rent to include the surplus return to all superior factors of production; but he held that land and capital had distinct economic characteristics which warranted keeping them as separate factors of production, and, thus, as distinct income sources.

Perhaps the main reason for the separation of land and capital is that the Peschian rent theory adopts in general the classical approach, being essentially a study of the share of the national income paid to the owners of land, in particular, of agricultural land. In its fulness it poses an even broader problem, investigating the sources of the income of the "agricultural entrepreneur" who is compared with his industrial counterpart and whose income is based on the same functions performed—except that in the agricultural enterprise the utility of the land is the most important income source (V, 701). Thus the analysis emphasizes the income derived from the yield of land.

It would be a misinterpretation of this emphasis, if it is thought Pesch considers the part of the income coming to the agricultural entrepreneur for the yield of the land as so distinct from the other founts that it can be mathematically determined.

[22] In the words of Haley: "There is to be noted a tendency to revert to the Paretian concept of rent, and to define it as the surplus return which an agent of production earns in a particular industry over and above its opportunity cost" (*ibid.*). This is a more restricted concept than that used by Pesch.

The product and its value result from the indissoluble co-operation of the different factors coming into consideration as causes or conditions for its production. Accordingly, the net return affords a reward not for the individual perform-ances isolated and marked off from each other, but for all taken together cumulatively. Consequently every search to mathematically distill out of the net income, as a real part, the share which in particular and alone falls to the owner of the property as a reward for making available the yield of the land must remain not only difficult but also without prospect (V, 702).

Rent is defined as "that part of net income which is espe-cially due to the land and its ownership" (V, 699). Or, more fully: "Land rent is that part of the entrepreneur's income which represents a compensation for the yield of the land, thus for the utility of the natural productivity of the land or other benefit of a particular land (especially its location)" (V, 701–702). Though this term is applicable to the return for the use of agricultural land, mines, and city property, Pesch limits his study for the most part to agricultural rent.

Since Pesch's definition of cost differs from "alternative" cost with its emphasis on competing use, he approaches in another way the most vexing problem in rent theory, namely, whether rent determines price, or vice versa.[23] It will be re-called that in the Peschian formula cost signifies the decrease in the value of the entrepreneur's wealth, because of the pay-ments necessary for production, and for which a recompense is expected from the sales price. But the yield of the soil in itself does not involve a decrease of the entrepreneur's wealth, and in this sense requires no recompense from the sales price, and thus does not fall under the concept of production cost.

[23] For an excellent historical discussion of the issues involved in this con-troversy, see Daniel Buchanan, "The Historical Approach to Rent and Price Theory," *Economica*, IX (June, 1929), pp. 123–55; also in *Readings in the Theory of Income Distribution*, pp. 599–637.

Rather the yield of the soil is a material performance of the property owner, and for making this yield available he receives a reward. It determines the price to the extent that it increases the utility of the product.

In the Peschian system, like the Ricardian, a distinction is made between absolute and relative rent. The former exists as soon as land becomes an economic good, and thus its yield has its own special value. It is found in every utilized land, it is rent *simpliciter*. "It bears a quasi-generic character, corresponds to the definition of land rent, and only receives its more proximate determination and specification through the greater fruitfulness, the favorable or unfavorable location of the piece of land, without its cause being reduced to this difference alone" (V, 703). On the other hand, relative or differential rent is a comparative concept, referring to the extra gain which results for this piece of land in comparison with another on account of special natural qualities important for production, or a special favorable location, etc. Relative rent presupposes the absolute rent.

The controlling thought here seems to be that absolute rent is the amount received by the marginal land, while superior land receives a relative or differential rent. For example, Pesch says that Ricardo is correct in that

> the landowner producing under the most unfavorable conditions obtains "no rent", i.e., no *differential* rent. There is lacking precisely the *extra gain* which is attributable to the special fruitfulness and better location. However, also in this case a yield from the land and consequently in the price of the product a return for this yield remains possible and perhaps is necessary. Though the *relative* rent is lacking, the *absolute* retains its value so long as even the less fruitful and more remote piece of land must be cultivated to cover a given market demand for its product (V, 707). (Italics in original.)

It may be helpful in order to clarify Pesch's theory of and attitude toward rent to compare it with Ricardo's. The Ricardian concept of absolute rent applies to a future possibility; that is, if all the land were already occupied and further additions of capital could no longer be profitably applied to the land, then the worst land, too would yield a rent (V, 705, note). The Peschian is a quasi-generic concept, something found in the yield of all lands. The Ricardian concept of relative or differential rent is limited to the income arising from the possession of land; Pesch—with most modern economists— extends its application to every income received because of a preferential position (V, 708, 714).

Though Pesch generalizes the application of relative rent, and his theory of costs resembles Say's "productive sources" [24] nevertheless he believes that land and capital are not essentially the same, and that absolute rent should be applied to land alone. For, in the production process land is a *causa principalis passiva,* while capital presents the conditions and *causa instrumentalis.* Also, there is a certain indestructibility about the soil: though it can be damaged by erosion, it cannot be used up. But factories and machines are used up until they are completely destroyed (V, 701).

The Ricardian position looks with disfavor upon rent; for it apprehends that the terminus of economic progress is the stationary state where the profit rate declines to zero, wages are at the physical minimum, and the rent from land, because of increasing costs, is high. Pesch asks:

[24] In reference to the development of profit theory in France compared to the English classical theory, Gordon remarks: "Say and his followers clearly demarcated between capitalist and entrepreneur and contributed, with some qualifications, a worth-while analysis of the productive functions of the latter" (*op. cit.,* p. 307, note 2). Pesch, however, did not follow Say in the distinction between capitalist and entrepreneur; on this point he is in the English classical tradition.

In reality was more income always taken from industry and accumulated by the property owners? Was the exclusive enrichment of the land owner and the impoverishment of the industrial entrepreneur historically true or a tenuous fiction? (V, 709–10).

Admitting the possibility for the *rate* of return on capital to decline, he points out that the *total amount* of the return may increase, if the amount of capital has become greater. Moreover, he concedes that the consequences of the Ricardian theory may perhaps be valid for a closed economy, but he believes they have no application in real circumstances.

For Pesch a high level of rent is a sign of favorable economic development. With a rising economy, population increases and becomes rich in buying power. Wants increase quantitatively and qualitatively. This increases the demand for the products of the land, a scarce factor, so its price (rent) increases. The reverse process takes place in a declining economy. However, this parallel movement of rent and economic development does not necessarily have to result. Other mitigating factors and influences diminish the effect, e.g., improvements in the technique of cultivation, foreign imports, etc. (V, 713). Nor should every rise in price be considered a disadvantage for the common welfare. As long as the buying power of the masses has increased at least correspondingly, higher prices can be absorbed; and if a suitable buying power is wanting, then even a low price for farm products may be an excessive burden. Also, the presence of a prosperous and productive agriculture is an advantage to industry and trade (V, 711).

Ultimately the objections against increased rents, inasmuch as they are due to the general economic phenomena of the rising cost of a scarce factor, are reduced to the question of the legitimacy of the right to private property. On this point there is no doubt in the mind of Pesch—though this social philosophic question need not be developed here. His attitude is well-expressed in his rejoinder to those who consider a rise in rents as due to an agrarian monopoly: ". . . it (private property) is still a good way, as long as a very considerable part of the people share in this apparent 'monopoly' " (V, 702).

4. Interest

In the modern interest controversies Pesch should be classified in the monetary camp as opposed to the real or natural; and amongst the monetarists he would take his place alongside of loanable-fund theorists rather than with the rigid liquidity-preference theorists.

For Pesch the interest on loans is the most important form of "pure" rent income, using "rent" here in the sense of an income received without labor on the basis of the possession of capital goods or claims. A loan is defined as "a credit transaction by which consumptible and fungible goods are transferred against the promise of a future restoration of an equal supply of the goods of the same type" (V, 716). Included under the term are both natural and monetary loans, but his analysis is concerned with monetary loans.[25]

Pesch accepted the label given his interest theory by his contemporaries, "the theory of economic performance or service" (V, 728). This theory was the subject of his first article published in 1888 in *Zeitschrift für katholische Theologie*,[26] and was incorporated, essentially unchanged, in the fifth volume of the *Lehrbuch* thirty-five years later. The essence of the Peschian position is that the modern interest rate is "the price, the equivalent, for a worth-while valuable service, i.e.,

[25] It is not easy to understand Harris' criticism: "The real nature of the services in the productive process is hidden from Pesch because he confuses money with capital" (*op. cit.*, p. 51). Pesch explicitly makes a clear distinction, see, e.g., III, 55–58.

[26] "Zinsgrund und Zinsgrenze," *op. cit.*, pp. 36–74, 393–418.

for the possibility of gaining a profit which with considerable generality is offered through the loan of a sum of money" (V, 728).

The concept of equivalence which was applied to price and the other factors of distribution is the key, also, for the proper understanding of Pesch's interest theory. And, it solves the apparent contradiction between the older church law and the present church praxis.[27]

To be a valuable service with a claim for an equivalent return, the opportunity for gain rendered by the loan must not be something personal—an opportunity which could be realized by the borrower alone—it must be a general economic phenomenon. In the medieval economy the opportunities for gain were confined to particular localities or persons.[28] Thus, the general condition was lacking which ensured that the lender rendered a service not due to the special circumstances

[27] At first glance it may seem that Pesch's treatment of interest theory over-emphasizes the "justification" aspect, and the Church's position in this matter. But as he explains: "We enter so fully into these reasons (why interest was forbidden in medieval times) since thereby the whole loan transaction is elucidated by assigning the interest under the principle of equivalence to the value of the service" (V, 716). It will be recalled that the principle of equivalence is not something introduced especially into the theory of interest, but was an important element in price theory and the exposition of the other distributive shares.

[28] In an almost forgotten passage John M. Keynes remarks on the characteristics of the medieval economy in reference to interest in similar fashion: ". . . As moralists they (the Canonists) were trying to devise general rules which would be applicable to the actual circumstances of experience. May not Mr. Somerville be right that the social evil of usury, as conceived by the Canonists, was essentially due to the fact that in the circumstances of their time saving generally went with the creation not of assets but of debts? In the Middle Ages the economic circumstances and magnitude of the risks did not favor capital enterprise, and the annual increment of capital wealth was negligible, zero or negative. Except where it was closely and directly associated with business or real estate (exceptions which they admitted), saving almost always had its counterpart in debt and not in assets; so that interest was generally 'usury.' The rate of interest at that time (as it is throughout the world today) was too high to permit an amount of enterprise on a scale equal to the current amount of positive saving." ("Saving and Usury," *Economic Journal*, XLII [March, 1932], pp. 136–37.)

of the borrower; and because of this interest was forbidden.

> Two facts establish a radical difference between the cir-
> cumstances of the medieval and later economy: (1) The in-
> comparably more important expansion of production and
> trade, whereby enormous sums were devoured by the growing
> enterprises. (2) The condition that anyone who had the neces-
> sary money available could participate in the business world
> for his own profit (V, 726).

This meant that in the modern economy the opportunity to
make a profit had become general. "In the whole economy productive investment became the prevailing employment of the
money supply, particularly of the amounts transferred in the
money market" (V, 727). By this, every loan included a special
effect which acquired a general exchange value; and hence
entitled the lender to demand an interest payment—for a
consequence regularly linked with the lending of money could
be designated as an effect of it.

> The real possibility of making a profit is caused by the mere
> availability of a greater monetary capital; and this availability
> is caused or brought about immediately by the lender's act of
> granting a loan. Thus the lender brings about the possibility
> of making a gain, which in the new circumstances is *per se*
> bound up with the availability of a greater supply of money,
> according to the old principle: "causa causae est causa causati"
> (*ibid.*).

To sum up, according to Pesch, interest is the equivalent
for a special service able to be valued in monetary terms. This
service is not due to a property of money, which in itself is
"barren" but is bound up with the loan on the grounds of
extrinsic circumstances.

It will be useful for the clarification of Pesch's thought, to
compare his with other theories, applied or applicable to
interest on monetary loans, and to observe his comments.

The "revenue theory" of Say, Knies, Menger, *et alii,* designates interest as a reward for the transferred *yield* of money. Pesch criticizes the theory as contrary to the nature of the loan contract: in a loan the ownership is transferred, not a mere yield.

The "productive theory" of Lauderdale, Carey, Walker, Molinari, v. Thünen, and others ascribes to money under modern economic conditions a special productivity. But money as a means of exchange and a measure of value is certainly not immediately productive. "That money brings to its possessor the possibility of making a gain arises not from a property of money,[29] is not due to a productivity proper to the money, but to the expansion of capitalistic production" (V, 728–29). The term "virtual productivity" of money, when analyzed merely says that under modern conditions the widespread possibility exists to apply the money to productive purposes. "But this is not a property of money with its primary functions . . ." (V, 729, note 1).

Böhm-Bawerk's time-preference theory sees the fundamental reason for interest in the difference in value between present and future goods—since the former have a higher value, the amount of future goods must be greater than the amount of present goods. Pesch's criticism is that the mere difference of time, considered alone, establishes no difference of value. The possibility of making a gain in the interval must be introduced; and to show this, Böhm-Bawerk's theory must have recourse to some other theory.

The "labor of saving" or "abstinence" theories of Senior, Bastiat, McCulloch, etc., consider interest as a wage for the "labor of saving" or a compensation for the "giving up" of the immediate enjoyment. Pesch wonders whether any borrower

[29] This aspect of Pesch's interest theory seems to have been overlooked by Harris, for he comments: "In this modern revision of scholastic interest theory, as stated by Pesch, gone is the old idea of the barrenness of money" *op. cit.,* p. 51).

is concerned how the lender acquired his money, whether by saving, inheritance, or even profiteering. The sacrifice element of the "abstinence" theory has a certain validity. A sacrifice required to make the loan entitles the lender to a recompense; but the generality and universal significance of this fact must be proved. In the modern economy with its income extremes there is reason to doubt that those who save make a great sacrifice by abstaining.

In reference to the theory that a loan for production is entitled to interest, but not a loan for consumption, Pesch contends that the whole approach is incorrect. It is not the purpose of the loan that is the crucial question, but whether the law of equivalence is satisfied. This looks to what has been loaned, not to what is to be done with what has been loaned.

Finally, Pesch's theory of performance presents a different formulation than the traditional scholastic theory.[30] The latter also makes the central fact of its formulation the modern economic phenomena of the general possibility of making a gain. Its explanation of the justification of demanding a return, however, is on the basis of *lucrum cessans*, i.e., that the interest is a substitute for the gain that eludes the lender because he granted the loan. Pesch explains the difference between the two formulae:

> This theory coincides in its real assumptions with our own. Its juridical formulation, however, may not be free from objection. As soon as one speaks of reimbursement for a damage or for loss of a gain, individual considerations immediately come to the fore. If it were a matter of determining the dam-

[30] Pesch does not present his particular formulation without adding the modest phrases, *"salvo meliore judicio"* (V, 728) and *"videant consules!"* (V, 731). See Oswald von Nell-Breuning's excellent comparison of the Peschian and the canonical theory of interest, "The Peschian Theory of Interest," *Social Order*, I (April, 1951), pp. 177–80. For an illuminating comparison of the doctrine of the late Medieval schoolmen (Molina, Lessius and Lugo) with modern interest theories, see Bernard W. Dempsey, *Interest and Usury* (London: Dobson, 1948).

age or loss of gain caused, for example, by a flood, we could not make a general appraisal applicable to all who suffer damage. We would have to determine in particular for each individual the amount of damage suffered or gain forgone. These considerations lead to no market price for the interest return; but modern interest appears in the form of a common price (V, 729).

Or, it may be said the traditional formula, akin to the abstinence theory, stresses the sacrifice of the lender because he gives up the money.[31] Pesch does not dispute this; but emphasizes the advantage to the borrower, the service rendered by the loan—and this service is not due to the personal opportunity of the borrower, but to a general economic circumstance.

It is to be regretted that Pesch did not offer a detailed analysis of the market process determining the rate of interest.[32] But he does state in summary fashion that the same factors determining the market price for other goods and services apply also to the loan market; and he does enumerate the main factors which are operative in interest rate determination. It will be noted in the following enumeration that all the essentials of the loanable fund theory are contained. The interest rate is determined "according to the *amount of money available and offered for the purpose of loans, the magnitude of the demand for loans, the magnitude of the gain* which usually can be made by means of the money, and the *general valuation of loans,* which again depends on the state and development of the economy" (V, 731). (Italics added.)

[31] The traditional theory in this regard is close to the Keynesian view as found in the *General Theory of Employment, Interest and Money* (New York: Harcourt, Brace and Co., Inc., 1936), esp. pp. 165–74. If it is correct that the traditional formula is similar to Keynes and the Peschian similar to the loanable fund theory, it is interesting to note how contemporary economists have reconciled these two approaches, see Haley, *op. cit.,* pp. 40–43.

[32] This hardly justifies Harris' statement: "But he fails to tell us how this level is determined or how a usurious loan is definitely to be recognized" (*op. cit.,* p. 47).

Also, there are particular factors, in addition to these general ones, which influence the height of the interest rate. These include the personal sacrifice of the lender, compensation for a profit foregone, a risk-premium, the conditions of the loan, the security offered, etc. These factors would have special reference to the problem of the variety of rates within *the* interest rate.

On the policy level, it would be an incorrect presumption to believe that Pesch looks to the state to fix interest rates. On the contrary, he points out that the consensus of economic literature has been unfavorable toward public interest rates. As he explains, if such legal rates were carried out strictly, they would operate to the harm of the national economy; and if there are only weak controls, the legal rate would soon become a phantom. Also, since there are so many special reasons to justify a departure from any general average rate, a legal rate based on the concept of such an average rate would lose all validity (V, 732).

Inasmuch as Pesch's interest theory and its justification of interest is based on a general phenomenon of the modern economy, he can make the statement: "With the transition to new forms and circumstances the question concerning the justification of interest may be presented anew for discussion" (V, 733).

CHAPTER SEVEN

CAPITALISM, SOCIALISM, AND THE SOCIAL SYSTEM OF LABOR

WHICH economic system can best fulfill the goal of the economy? Capitalism as we know it today? A modified capitalism? Socialism? This is the concern of the present chapter with particular attention to the organizational principle of these possible economic systems. The discussion will be on two levels: as a question of alternative economic systems, and of the philosophic systems upon which they are based. This distinction is important because there is a close relationship between an economy and the philosophy which motivates it and because the two levels of discussion do not contain neat parallel categories.

On the philosophic level the contrasts are between individualism, socialism, and solidarism. The economic systems considered are capitalism, socialism, and the Peschian social system of labor.[1] The relationship existing between the categories

[1] To certain people this proposition will appear meaningless, if not false, for they posit a false dichotomy between capitalism and socialism. As B. S. Keirstead phrases it: ". . . the issue of socialism and serfdom versus capitalism and democracy is a false and misleading issue, because the alternatives are not

of the two levels and within each level may be briefly summarized. Individualism, socialism, and solidarism are mutually
exclusive. Also the solidaristic system of labor and socialism, as
an economic system, are mutually exclusive. But since individualism and capitalism are not *per se* inevitably linked together,
the Peschian economic system and capitalism, taken in certain
senses, are not incompatible. For the present it may be stated
that the solidaristic economic system may be conceived as
operating in a framework of capitalism as this term is usually
understood in current literature.

The close inter-relationship between the organization of
the economy and social philosophy is emphasized by Pesch.
Every economist who desires that welfare be shared by all at
least tacitly accepts some principle or fundamental norm as
the foundation of social life. But these economists

> are not of the same mind if the question is raised in which
> way, especially, through which type of organization of the
> economy such a condition is to be realized. In particular, the
> decisive and distinguishing point is how is the relation of
> the individual to the whole with respect to the common wel-
> fare to be fashioned, e.g., whether he can work unhindered
> as a free individual, or whether he is to become important
> in the economic sphere merely as a member or "associate" of
> the whole. Therefore we will have to investigate to which or-
> ganizational form and, corresponding to it, to which principle
> of organization priority is due (I, 279).

This issue may be restated in terms of what should be the
unifying principle of the economy, or the principle of *order*
in the economy. Or, again, it may be viewed as a search for a
principle which offers "a balance of the individual interests,
harmony between the individual well-being and the common
well-being, freedom in and with order . . ." (I, 280).

---

historically genuine!" ("The Conditions of Survival," *American Economic Review*, XL, Proceedings [May, 1950], p. 435.)

In the following sections first will be offered a brief explanation of the background philosophies, then will follow an analysis of the respective economic systems to which they are applied. Finally, the particular problem of the "vocational groups" will be considered.

1. Social Philosophies: Individualism, Socialism, and Solidarism

The main emphasis in this consideration of the philosophies of individualism, socialism, and solidarism will be on Pesch's solidarism. The discussion of the other two social principles is primarily to bring out the differences that exist between them and solidarism. The issues which arise, though of a socio-political nature, are still economically significant, for "it is self-evident that the type of unity which in general characterizes the political society is also of distinct importance for this part of the social life which we call the economy" (I, 271).[2]

The guiding idea of individualism is the *absolute* freedom and independence of economic individuals seeking their own ends. Opposed to this individualistic decentralization, socialism demands a completely unified, centralized, economic society with the abolishment of all social differences between classes and professions. Solidarism is a middle system "which properly asserts the solidaristic union of men—whether considered simply as men or as members of the natural communities, the family and the state" (I, 432). In this system unity is

[2] Cf. Wright's statement as quoted in Howard S. Ellis, "Research as Seen in *A Survey of Contemporary Economics," American Economic Review*, XXXIX, Proceedings (May, 1949), p. 439, where this Peschian proposition seems to be the implicit foundation of Wright's advice: "We should, therefore, try to see how many of the evils of our present system inhere in it and how many are the results of social organization as such."

harmonized with multiplicity, order with freedom. Its guiding thought is the notion of the common welfare: "the full carrying out of the idea of the community" (IV, 208). Nevertheless Pesch can claim "solidarism proceeds from the individual and society *together* so that to each is assigned what belongs to them: *from men in the midst of society*" (II, 238). (Italics in original.)

The difference between these three mutually exclusive social philosophies can be seen in the context of the central problem of the concept of society and, thus, of the individual and his relation to the social whole, particularly as manifested in the economic sphere of social life.

Individualism sees in society no real unit. What it calls "society" is a mere mechanism, the interplay of the actions of individuals seeking their own ends; or it is a mere sum of economic relations. It postulates a natural order based on unrestrained freedom, on whose unhindered effect the welfare of all depends. The national economy is viewed as a sum of isolated units, which are bound together only by the mind into a logical unity, or appear linked together by mere exchange relationships (I, 272; II, 264). Also the state is a mere sum of isolated individuals. Its function is conceived as that of a "night watchman" whose task is to protect the individual persons and their property.[3]

[3] What this individualistic theory of the state means for the theory of public finance is brought out clearly by Pesch: "The state must create security which protects the owners in the possession, increase, and enjoyment of their material wealth. In return for this these will and should then bear their share of the cost which the creation of this security occasions. From this point of view the *obligation of the taxes and the distribution of the tax burden* is evaluated. According to this the individual stands *vis-à-vis* the state merely in an exchange relationship. In the exact measure as the citizen enjoys benefits from the political institutions, is determined the burden of taxes which he must bear. . . . Thus taxation in equal proportion is represented as the only just distribution of the tax burden (equivalence or interest theory). Similar is the view of taxes as a security premium (security theory), which also wishes to distribute the tax according to the quantity of the goods protected, proportional to the magnitude of the wealth (Thiers)" (I, 305). (Italics in original.)

How in the solidaristic system taxes are to be measured by the capacity to

This individualism, as manifested in the economic theory and policy of the classical school, is described by Pesch:

> It prefers to seek "exact" laws, to deal with sensible percep-
> tion, with interior and external observation rather than with
> principles, to deal with social and economic "phenomena"
> rather than with the free actions of morally and legally re-
> sponsible men, etc. Accordingly, if nothing is to be expected
> from a reasonable planned reform—which must disturb the
> operation of "nature," must violate the "natural" law, the
> "natural" order—then nothing remains but that the over-
> coming of social and economic abuses is to be expected only
> from the unhindered effect of the natural factors, from the
> freest development of individuality. . . . Now and hence-
> forward the state is to be limited to the protection of persons
> and properties, the protection of the free contract (I, 438–39).

In socialism the concept of the unity in society is distorted. The collective society which it requires presents the unity of "oneness" rather than a union of the many. The individual is only an "associate," not an autonomous personality. The economy becomes a single, great collective unit with the society as the sole owner of the means of production, the sole director of production, and the judge of its distribution. No recognition is offered to the "natural" rights of the individual and the family. Private ownership of the means of production and competition in the economic sphere are suppressed. It seeks equality of economic conditions for all; and freedom would cease to be a privilege of the ruling class. But observes Pesch:

> Whether equality and freedom may be joined together so
> easily, whether the equality of subjection under the sole

---

pay of the citizen, based on the principle of the citizen's duty to the whole,
see I, 455, note 2. For a fuller treatment of Pesch's theory of public finance, see
Heinrich Lechtape, *Die Frage Steuergerechtigkeit* (Grundsätzliches zur Finanzreform auf Grund des Solidaritätssystems von Heinrich Pesch, S.J.) (Freiburg
im Br.: Herder, 1920).

absolute ruler, "society," can guarantee freedom for all, whether the equality of economic conditions may be maintained in the long run without the continual suppression of the inequalities constantly emerging from the natural differences of individuals are enigmas whose solution may not be so easy for socialism (I, 439).

Solidarism postulates the metaphysical equality of all men, while it recognizes the differences found in the concrete physical individuals (II, 238). It considers men as part of a moral "organism, a real unity among members different among themselves, who are bound together through a common purpose and an inner principle" (I, 272). Thus, there is offered unity without a denial of the multiplicity of members with their individual autonomy. This unity is described as of a "moral-organic" character. In terms of the economy, its configuration is said to bear:

> 1. an organic character in a twofold sense: first as a name for the relationship of the individual economies to the whole, then with reference to the organic-systematical construction of the economic vocations;
> 2. a moral character, insofar as the economic subjects are morally bound to adapt their endeavors to the order governed by the *finis* of the state;
> 3. a moral—not physical—organic character, since the economic subjects are precisely free men, whose own end and autonomy claim proper recognition (I, 437).

Briefly, in solidarism, the economy is an organic-moral unity of many autonomous economic units bound together through the goal and the authority of society. It is a community of free citizens laboring for the true common economy, not in the sense of the communistic compulsory economy but through the subordination of the individual economies to the national economic task of providing for the needs of the whole of the people—"a providing for needs, which does not exclude the market economy as does the communistic covering-of-needs economy" (II, 265). The variety, freedom, particular aims, autonomy, and self-responsibility of private enterprise are not suppressed. The role of the state here is more than that of a "night watchman"; it is to direct, supervise, stimulate, and restrain the activities of the individual economic units insofar as the common welfare demands it (I, 276).[4] Trenchantly Pesch describes the rights and place of the individual in the solidaristic community:

> No system emphasizes more strongly than this (solidarism) that the individual is not a mere member of a whole, mere means for the goal of all, but that he is an end in himself. Men have . . . as men in themselves, natural tasks and goals and, consequently, natural rights: the right to exist, the right to work, to acquire property, to activate their personal capabilities, the right to found a family, etc. Positive law may be concerned with the more proximate determination of the exercise of these rights. The right itself, however, precedes every positive law and cannot be suppressed by it (I, 440).

Again let it be emphasized that the stress on the importance of the objective goal of the economy does not set aside private enterprise's predominant profit motive. It merely insists that this private, subjective motive cannot be the guiding rule for the whole economy; rather all economic striving receives its higher social significance from the economy's goal (I, 280).

To put the problem more generically, solidarism does not expect, nor does it require, that all men will be benevolent and that all motives of self-interest must be abolished.[5] Self-interest, as noted above,[6] is a natural instinct which could

---

[4] For a complete treatise on the economic role of the state, see III, 744–78 and IV, 202–36.

[5] As Oswald v. Nell-Breuning has so tersely put it: "The vocational order does not require that men be angels" ("Berufsständische Ordnung," *Stimmen der Zeit*, CXLIII [Heft 4, 1949], p. 261).

[6] See Chapter II, pages 41–42.

hardly be eradicated, even if one wished to do so. If altruism were established as the principle of society this would be "a dream, an illusion of phantasy, not a system which could satisfy the realities of life" (II, 266). What is required is that the instinct of self-interest be regulated and ordered so that both the individual and the community are satisfied.

It is most important to investigate the place of freedom in the solidaristic philosophy not only because of the prominence of this issue in economic literature but also because it is rather commonly believed that solidarism postulates an authoritarian system with no or little consideration for economic freedom. At least it cannot be denied that Pesch is aware of the problem.[7] He says that the great problem for theory and practice, which constitutes the object of the research of the economist and of the toil of the statesman is: "How order the activities of the different factors without the elimination of freedom, of economic independence, without the suppression of competition?" (II, 214).[8]

Solidarism disavows absolute freedom in the economic sphere just as it rejects a compulsory planned economy. And it is illogical to suppose that one must choose either of these extremes. The Peschian middle system holds that unlimited, unrestrained freedom can be seriously harmful to the attaining of the goal of the economy. At the same time it recognizes in freedom "a major, stimulating motive animating the development of abilities; thus it demands and protects every freedom which is in harmony with the common welfare and which can further the most favorable possible attainment of the goal of

[7] For a review of Pesch's frequent application of freedom to economic problems see my "Economic Freedom in Pesch," *Social Order,* I (April, 1951), pp. 161–68.

[8] See Keirstead, *op. cit.,* p. 444, for a similar expression of the problem: "The real questions have to do with the most appropriate controls, the minimum administrative apparatus necessary for their implementation, and the constitutional devices necessary to ensure that administrative power is never arbitrary or irresponsible."

the economy" (II, 245). It is the goal of the economy which ultimately determines the measure of individual freedom. The latter will, accordingly, vary in different circumstances; individual economic freedom is an elastic concept.

For those who wish to make freedom an end in itself many practical problems remain insolvable except on the basis of expediency which builds no firm foundation as a rational guide. Pesch adopts the more realistic position that if freedom is not to become the base instrument of brutal self-seeking it must postulate a higher standard. This higher standard is justice. And only the acceptance of the principle of authority develops and guarantees that degree of justice without which freedom remains only a parody.[9] One practical conclusion from this analysis of the freedom concept is that the higher we value freedom, the more must we seek justice (II, 267).

It is clear from his writings that Pesch was conscious of the misunderstanding of his position. He points to his hierarchy of regulating factors (first, the conscience of men; second, self-governing vocational groups; third, the state—and in that order) as a manifestation of how high he esteems freedom. He adds:

> Then I have marked freedom as a constituent of national welfare, although not the wild freedom of arbitrariness, but the freedom of order. I have put down free enterprise as the rule, public enterprise as the exception. I have said: Every freedom of economic trade is justified, which is consistent with the goal of the economy, with the material welfare of the people. Further than this no man can go in the demand for freedom (II, ix–x).[10]

[9] Cf. Keirstead's: "Freedom consists of purposeful action, and implies, in all social processes, an intelligent understanding of these processes and purposeful direction of them and control over them. A society which suffers from an unwanted depression is not a fully free society. . . . Thus freedom necessitates adequate public control over the social process" (*ibid.*, pp. 443–44).

[10] Hardly in keeping with this is the (it is to be hoped) facetious remark of

A related and parallel problem is the question of private property. Like individualism solidarism recognizes the right of private ownership of property. But it is opposed to an absolute, irresponsible concept of private ownership, just as it rejects the socialistic concept of state ownership of all the means of production or the communistic state ownership of all property. Solidarism clarifies the limits of private ownership by introducing the requirements proceeding from a social duty. The central notion of property is that "the goods of the earth should serve all mankind" (II, 243). And it is recognized that this goal is best attained through private ownership subordinate to higher rights.

Thus solidarism holds: (1) Property signifies power, but limited power subordinate to the moral and legal order. (2) Property is a right, but not the highest right that would place the material world above the world of men. (3) Property is not an end in itself, but a means to an end—namely, the ordered providing for the needs of all men living in society (II, 242–43).

The social duty of the property owner embraces more than charity providing for the individual needs of the poor, or the obligation to pay taxes. It implies also the duty to use one's property for the furthering of the common welfare.

> It does not remain within the whim of landowners to leave the land unused, if its utilization is needed to cover the wants of the people. This is equally true of the means of production available for other production spheres which are needed to keep production going and to perfect it. The duty of the property owners and the duty of the state stand in the sharpest conceivable opposition to an anarchistic production (II, 244).

Wright: "The right to make a fool of oneself is one of the most precious aspects of democracy!" ("The Economics of a Classless Society," *American Economic Review*, XXXIX, Proceedings [May, 1949], p. 34.)

In the last resort the state has the right and duty to see that
the property is used for the benefit of the common welfare.

2. Extreme Economic Systems: Individualistic Capitalism and Socialism

The controversy about the alternative economic systems is
between capitalism, socialism, and the social or solidaristic
system of labor. The connecting link with the social philosophic discussion in the preceding section is via the respective
principles of organization upon which these economic systems
are based.

> Corresponding to our social philosophic distinction between
> individualism, socialism, and solidarism we assume three gen-
> eral organizational principles for the economy: (1) the in-
> dividualistic principle of freedom and self-interest of normally
> isolated autonomous economic subjects; (2) the socialistic
> principle of direct authoritarian control of the economic
> process on a collective basis; (3) the solidaristic principle
> which, on the basis of the responsibility to the community
> (a norm binding on both citizens and public authorities)
> arising from the social end of the people united in a political
> community, determines, measures, and limits the freedom,
> private property, and self-interest of the autonomous subjects
> and their associations, and likewise the authority of the state
> . . . (I, 451).

The inter-relationship between these organizational principles is that the individualistic principle excludes collectivism and requires private enterprise, but is in itself no principle of order and to this extent is incompatible with solidarism.
The socialistic principle seeking a collective formation of economic life with the suppression of the private economic order
clashes with both of the other principles. Finally, the solidar-

istic principle rejects both the collective economy and the mechanism of the individualistic, private economic order. "It requires private property in the means of production, the private economic organization, but with 'true organization,' i.e., with a moral-organic order ruled by the requirements of the common welfare" (I, 452).

Unless the comparison of the various economic systems is to be hopelessly involved in confusion, it is imperative that the various senses in which the term "capitalism" is used— particularly by Pesch—be clear. First, he refers to "capitalistic production," the technical fact of a rather intensive use of produced means of production. This is a technical condition which would be found in any modern progressive economic system. Second, reference is made to the "capitalistic enterprise," the type of organization in which normally today capitalistic production is carried on. This business form assumes a social order in which there is private ownership of capital goods and assumes the presence of a laboring force which cooperates in production under the guidance of the capitalistic entrepreneur. The essence of the capitalistic enterprise lies in this that "the means of production are acquisitive wealth of the owner and that the production is executed at the risk and under the direct or indirect guidance of the capitalistic entrepreneur" (IV, 561). Capitalism in this sense is excluded by socialism but is consistent with the social system of labor, though it is not essential to it. "The 'capitalism' with which we here contrast the social system of labor is not 'capitalism' in the designated two-fold sense: thus not technical capitalism, not the ownership of capital as such, the private economic organization as such" (II, 227).

The third sense in which capitalism is used by Pesch is as "the embodiment of certain abuses which arose in the historical development of the capitalistic enterprise, specifically in the 'capitalistic epoch,' but which are not essential to the capi-

talistic enterprise and are not found in every capitalistic enterprise" (IV, 561–62). Reference is primarily to the "spirit" of
capitalism based fundamentally on an exaggerated individualism. It is thus more accurately defined:

> *An economic system arising from the individualistic freedom*
> *of striving for gain, ruled by the principles of exchange and*
> *the practices of the liberal economic epoch, serving in the*
> *first line not the whole welfare of the people, but the owner*
> *of capital and his money interests* (II, 230). (Italics in original.)

It requires a free economy whose successful operation is expected solely from the self-regulation by the market. It advocates a *laissez-faire* policy by the state.

Capitalism in this sense may best be called "individualistic
capitalism." Here "the enterprise itself has become the goal
and the end of the economic system" (III, 60).

> The providing for the needs of the people is less the task of
> the economy than a means for the enrichment of private
> enterprise. The subjective goal of private acquisitiveness is
> elevated above the objective task of the national economy.
> The private economy dominates the national (II, 227).

This type of capitalism is criticized not only because it is
based on a false social philosophy but, more to the point here,
also because of the social and economic evils to which it has
led. Among these are mentioned: ". . . the overthrow of the
middle class, the destruction of the less strong competitors,
concentration of the possession of capital, wealth in the hands
of the few, the exploitation of the consumers and the proletariat workers" (II, 227). Some of the more specific charges are
that it causes or permits unemployment, excessive speculation,
limitless competition which leads to monopoly, and irresponsible advertising.[11] It is admitted that this "free" capitalism was

[11] Cf. the discussion of Pesch's position on competition in chapter V, section 2.

able to develop and contribute to an increase in production, but it is claimed that it was not suited for the proper distribution of the goods purchased.

Fundamentally, Pesch's criticism is against the individualistic organizational principle which has caused individualistic capitalism to lack unity, a coherent task for the economy as a whole, and consequently, regulating principles for the economic sphere, as well as regulating factors.

This fundamental approach is reflected in Pesch's view on the cause of crises.[12] He sums up his analysis briefly: "Not the private ownership of the means of production, but the defective regulation of economic life is in fact the fundamental cause of the great disturbances of the economic process" (V, 786). Some appreciation of his position can be acquired from the program recommended for the state in order to combat depressions:

> It (the state) can through its security laws lessen the worst abuses of stock promotions, and can combat the abuse of thoughtless granting of credit, it can place a restraint on the great central-note banks through a proper discount policy of an artificial advance. Also the management of credit and stock banks requires a regulating law (regulation of deposits, of acceptance and account credits). Truthfulness, honesty, and reliability also can be influenced by law and government. We are thinking of the correct determination of stock exchange arrangements, of the combatting of abusive stock speculation, the abuses of mortgage banks, etc. Finally, the laws protecting labor, security for labor, labor exchanges, relief works, the postponement of large orders to depression times, etc., dampen the effects of a depression (V, 787).

The term "socialism" does not present the same difficulty as the term "capitalism," though a few clarifying observations

---

[12] It seems better to call Pesch's brief exposition on business cycles "views" rather than a "theory," for his ideas are not developed.

are called for. In the wide sense socialism embraces both the system favoring public ownership only of the means of production (socialism *stricte dicta*) and the system demanding public proprietorship of both producers' and consumers' goods (communism). As the term is generally used by Pesch it refers to both socialism in the strict sense and communism (I, 324–25).[13] From one aspect, socialism can be viewed as one of a heterogeneous series of proposed economic systems or programs which have as a common note the rule of the economy by the state. The leading units of this series are: communism and socialism seeking state ownership of property; a planned economy under state control; and nationalization. After the presentation of Pesch's criticism of socialism as an economic system, his views on a planned economy and nationalization will be briefly considered.

From an economic point of view, Pesch's general criticism of socialism is that it attempts to solve the evils of individualistic capitalism by introducing more serious errors. He does not hold the absolute impossibility of a socialistic order. But he believes it cannot long endure. One reason is because it imposes superhuman tasks on the central planning board. Since in Pesch's time the Lange-Taylor "competitive" solution to von Mises' generally accepted "impossibility" argument had not yet appeared, and the Barone-Pareto foundation of the later Lange-Taylor position, though extant, was not widely known, it may be profitable to digress for a moment to examine this new competitive solution.

Lange's position does not seem to have solved all the prob-

---

[13] See Joseph A. Schumpeter, "The March into Socialism," *American Economic Review*, XL, Proceedings (May, 1950), p. 448, footnote, where it is stated that socialism and communism, barring the Russian angle, should be used synonymously. See also his *Capitalism, Socialism, and Democracy* (2nd ed.; New York: Harper, 1947), p. 168, where he states that if he had to use the terms "collectivism" and "communism" he should make them synonymous with socialism.

lems for an economic theory of socialism. The main problems noted by Bergson,[14] for example, are: (1) managerial controls, though they may not be as great as Hayek supposes; (2) rigidities and undue standardization; (3) inequality of income, which he feels may be greater than Lange supposes. One important feature of the competitive solution which has not been stressed and is in danger of being overlooked is that the issue is not whether theoretically socialism *can* work but whether it will *be permitted* to work. A crucial difference between competition in socialism and in capitalism is that competition is an *automatic* determining factor in the capitalistic system—it inheres in the system. In socialism competition is not automatic, it must be introduced *ab extra,* and no absolute guarantee is offered that it will be introduced. This arbitrariness is revealed in Lange's description of the production process under socialism:

> The decisions of the managers of production are no longer guided by the aim of maximizing profit. Instead certain rules *are imposed* on them by the Central Planning Board which aim at satisfying consumers' preferences in the best way possible.[15]

Again it is found in Bergson's description: "Each production unit is *instructed* to conduct its operation in accord with two basic rules." [16] But what guarantee is there that the instructions will be given or the rules imposed? And even if they are, what guarantee have we that the managers will follow them? A possible "reward" solution, if the rules should be imposed, merely

14 "Socialist Economics," *A Survey of Contemporary Economics, op. cit.,* pp. 434–40.

15 "On the Economic Theory of Socialism," in B. Lippincott, ed., *On the Economic Theory of Socialism* (Minneapolis: Minnesota, 1948), p. 75. (Italics added.)

16 *Op. cit.,* pp. 432–33. Another confirmation of this view of the competitive solution is found in Bergson's careful statement, *"Assuming* that the socialist economic system *were* administered in accord with the very general principles and procedures outlined . . ." (*ibid.,* p. 434). (Italics added.)

reduces the problem to a further, more general problem of "inequality of incomes."

This inevitability of unequal incomes is another reason why Pesch believes a socialistic system cannot be permanent. Men have been endowed by nature with different gifts, temperaments, and talents; and if a new property class is not to arise, then compulsion and injustice must be employed in order that each individual is *not* paid what is due him.[17] It is not the immorality of the injustice that Pesch emphasizes here, but that injustice and compulsion are not conducive to economic efficiency or political stability (II, 232; I, 389). And, as Wright points out, even if there were equality of wealth, the problem of inequality of power would not be solved: "We do not have a choice between a world of complete equality and a world of inequality."[18]

Moreover, cites Pesch, the socialist economy is based on a false psychology. Common property is not normally utilized as efficiently as private property. "Production requires an initiative which today is supplied by the entrepreneur but which cannot be acquired in a social production" (I, 387). And, even on a broader scale, there is lacking every personal incentive to exert oneself, since every opportunity for social and economic betterment remains closed. For many men indulgence blocks the way to ambition; and only the competition of daily life compels them to exert themselves. The economist

---

[17] Lange touches upon this dilemma, but does not offer any satisfactory solution. There is no reason to believe that the cases of a disproportion between the value of the marginal product of the services of labor and the marginal disutility of the work are rare. Cf. Bergson, *op. cit.,* p. 437: "Our impression is that these exceptions might be more numerous than is commonly assumed, e.g., what of the personnel in high level jobs in the bureaucracy?" It is not clear, however, how Lange's (and Bergson's) high tax to equalize disposable income can be levied without any adverse effect on the supply of these services. Also Bergson's point about the intra-marginal workers seems a telling argument against equalitarian socialism.

[18] "Prospects for Capitalism," *A Survey of Contemporary Economics, op. cit.,* p. 462.

who thinks that "a love for a general economic society" will inspire them "must be a poor psychologist" (*ibid.*).[19] Moreover, "economic independence is an essential part of civilian freedom"; and only a brutal tyranny will be able to continually repress this natural instinct (*ibid.*).

Another problem is: who will guide the socialistic economic society? Proletarian dictatorship and socialism belong together" (II, 233). There will still be class egoism and class rule; but with the players exchanging roles. And, even if there should be a genuine election, the representatives would not be chosen unanimously, but would be a majority imposing on the minority decisions affecting their daily private life.

Closely akin to socialism is the proposal of a planned economy,[20] which is necessarily involved in socialism, though theoretically every planned economy does not involve socialism. Nevertheless, like socialism, a planned economy is rejected in theory and practice by Pesch. Fundamentally, it is

[19] Cf. Wright, "The Economics of a Classless Society," *op. cit.*, pp. 34–35; M. M. Bober (Discussion), "The Sociology and Economics of Class Conflict," *American Economic Review*, XXXIX, Proceedings (May, 1949), p. 43.

[20] A planned economy (*Planwirtschaft*) should not be confused with economic planning (*Wirtschaftplanung*). The former is involved immediately with decisions usually associated with private enterprise; the latter is concerned with setting the proper economic environment so that private enterprise can make its own decisions. Cf. Nell-Breuning, "Um die 'Berufsständische Ordnung,'" *Stimmen der Zeit,* CXLII (Heft 7, 1948), p. 15: "Christian social theory can see in a planned economy only an evil—in certain circumstances a necessary evil. In opposition to a planned economy it advocates the idea of economic planning." Also, cf. Ellis, "The Economic Way of Thinking," *op. cit.*, p. 12, for the substance of the thought: "Some planning is, and some is not, compatible with the maximizing of the field of individual free choice. Some planning signifies the formation of institutions such as the International Monetary Fund, which was designed—at least in some notable respects—to restore free-market processes. Planning in another sense, such as the agricultural price-parity program, is well calculated to undermine market processes and make the economy subject solely to political forces. . . . It is impossible to oppose "planning" if it simply means forethought, consistency, and rational provision for contingencies in public policy; but very often the term simply covers the growth of political decisions at the expense of the economic calculus." Also, cf. Sumner H. Slichter, "Long Term Economic Trends," *American Economic Review*, XL, Proceedings (May, 1950), p. 468.

opposed to the principle of subsidiarity which requires that a higher social organization should not undertake what a social organization, lower in the scale, can do at least equally well. "Because of the complexity of conditions any such central direction (by the state) would lose at its highest levels a view of the whole picture and would not be able to do what innumerable, self-interested entrepreneurs are in a position to accomplish" (I, 200). Nor would a planned economy be able to increase production. "An absorption and 'sucking out' of the independence of the entrepreneur caused by the 'planned-economy' is entirely unsuited to lead to an increase of the productive power of the economy" (IV, 539). Also, a planned economy is viewed as a transitional form leading to socialism.

The final form of state control to be considered is the complex case of nationalization. Pesch distinguishes two types of nationalization:

> It is not the same thing, if it clearly and unequivocally is said: "The taking-over by the state of an economic field in itself does not belong to the task, the goal of the state, but is only an exceptional justified means"; or if such a venture is reckoned within the sphere of the function of the state (II, 210–11).

The latter, nationalization on principle, is rejected since it exceeds the normal legitimate function of the state. The former, *ad hoc* nationalization is not condemned, but each case is to be judged by rather definite criteria.

The fundamentals of Pesch's position are drawn from the principle of subsidiarity and the goal of the economy.

> On principle, private property and private enterprise may not be suppressed in any sphere where its effective continuance can satisfy the common welfare. Rather, only according to the postulates of social justice does a limitation of freedom take place: a substitution of private enterprise by

the public enterprise takes place exclusively, solely, and only, in such sectors where indubitably the national economic need in reference to the whole rightly demands the suppression of a private enterprise incapable, unsuited or harmful to the needs of the national economy (I, 198–99).

The practical question always to be asked is whether the nationalization of this particular industry is possible, necessary, and impellingly suitable. And before a nationalization program is approved it must be clear that it is *essentially* better from the technical, economic, financial, and social aspect.

Pesch sums up his general position on nationalization:

> Thus, again we here take a middle position between individualism and socialism. We reject as one-sided exaggeration the socialistic demand of exclusively public business. But no less superficial would it be if every public enterprise were designated simply as economically of little value and were dismissed as incompatible with the prosperity of the economy (IV, 212).

It is instructive to study more closely the arguments and criteria Pesch offers for and against *ad hoc* nationalization, since it throws light not only on this topic but also on his general view of the economic process. The thumb rule is that industries which depend on individual initiative and decisions, and which require adaptability are not promising for nationalization. On the other hand, those industries able to be directed more schematically and bureaucratically may be even more productive under public control than if left in private hands. Where the speculative factor is strong and quick mobility is required, public ownership will always be less suitable than private. In general, mass production industries would appear more suited for nationalization than other sections of the economy.

The arguments in favor of public ownership are: where abuses exist because of a monopoly position, these can be remedied; the public industry has greater credits at its disposal, and thus can undertake greater risks; advertising costs can be reduced; prices can be stabilized; the needs of customers can be more effectively evaluated; crises can be dampened by stockpiling in times of depression; better care can be taken of the workers. The main argument against nationalization is that "in a public business the personal interest of the entrepreneur is lacking; and its effectiveness cannot be fully substituted for by any means or method" (IV, 215). Also, self-responsibility and willingness to take risks would decline, technical progress would be weakened or restricted, bureaucracy with its prejudices and meddlesomeness would rise.

To sum up the Peschian position on nationalization: this is "the last means, which is to be applied only if the vocational-group or state regulation does not suffice to eliminate the abuses of private enterprise" (IV, 212).

3. The Middle Way: The Social System of Labor

Rather than individualistic capitalism or socialism, Pesch proposes the solidaristic or social system of labor. It is an economic system for it is concerned with the organization of the economy. And it is a new economic system, "since it gives to the Smithian industrial system a *solidaristic* foundation through the social regulation of the economic process" (II, 214). And while it is considered a practical plan, it does not claim to offer the key to the immediate solution of every economic problem (III, 62).

Since individualistic capitalism with its *laissez-faire* policy requires no institutional implementation but rather implies a negation of it, the social system of labor proposing the corporate or vocational organizations may easily be misconceived as seeking and consisting in merely an external institutional reform. But it is a wider concept than this; and in a two-fold sense. First, it stresses "the whole regulative and constructive significance of the solidaristic principle for the ordering and shaping" of the economy (I, 444). This has reference to the action of the state, of the vocational and other groups, and of individuals in the ordering of economic life. Second, more fundamental and considered more important, the Peschian system is founded on, embraces, and requires a "spirit"—an ideology, aspiration, or attitude—without which neither this economic system nor any other can succeed.[21]

This spirit, essential to the success of the economy, is the desire for the common good based on the organic concept of society. A three-fold solidarity is implied—that of mankind in general, of the citizens within a given state, and of all engaged in a particular vocation. The intangibleness of the notion of a "spirit" does not make it less important.[22] For example, Professor Schumpeter's pessimistic conclusions regarding capitalism in his *Capitalism, Socialism, and Democracy* are based on the premise of an insuperably hostile ideology.[23]

Essential to the implementation of the proper attitude toward the community is the vocational organization of the economy. The vocational groups may be described in general

[21] It will be recalled that "Geist" is prominent in Sombart's analysis of capitalism. See F. L. Nussbaum's bibliographical article, "The Economic History of Renaissance Europe," *Journal of Modern History* (Dec., 1941), pp. 529–31. Incidentally, Nussbaum says that "Geist" is a "term which the American and English have been slow to use and awkward in using" (*ibid.*, p. 529).

[22] Cf. B. S. Keirstead, "The Condition of Survival," *op. cit.*, p. 436: "These are economic questions. More important are the political and moral questions. . . . Have the attitudes, the social beliefs and myths and ideals associated with what we call capitalism the kind of moral quality which survives?"

[23] See Wright, "Prospects for Capitalism," *A Survey of Contemporary Economics,*" *op. cit.*, pp. 471–72. Wright doubts Schumpeter's pessimistic conclusions, since this is not a question of an inexorable law, "but rather of the degree of intelligence exercised in future economic policy."

as vocational communities: organizations embracing all engaged in a particular profession or performing a particular service for the nation. All with the same function in society, even though they have different interests between themselves, belong to the same group. The vocational communities are organs of society, which operate as the representatives of the interests of the group and as self-governing authorities for the particular profession or industry. For the perfect fulfillment of their task they must be conscious of the importance of the national interest, and they must cooperate with other vocational groups and with organizations within their particular profession which are concerned with their own particular interests, e.g., employer and employee organizations.

The vocational organization of the economy is considered a need of every age—but not in the sense as if it is essential to the existence of the political society, as if it is required by the natural law. Rather is it a *proprium:* something without which the political society cannot reach the fullness of its perfection (IV, 263). Nor is any one historical form of a vocational organization considered applicable to all epochs. The particular type needed will vary according to economic, social, and political conditions. For example, the guilds (a type of vocational organization) belong to a past age (II, 220). The modern group is expected to be more mobile, more flexible, more specialized, while still being more comprehensive.

The industrial framework of these social organs is not described in detail by Pesch. As he explains:

> Certainly prudence restrains the theorist from rashly tying himself to a definite form of organization, etc. Rather the theorist will limit himself to this: to exhibit the course of a sound development, to sketch the broadest outlines for its further development, to designate the framework. But he leaves the filling in of these with concrete details to the wis-

dom and prudence of the better trained and more experienced man of practice (II, ix).

In keeping with this prudent observation Pesch offers merely the bare skeleton of the framework of the vocational organizations. Three levels are indicated; a local substructure, a district organization in which employers and employees meet together, and a supreme national economic council (IV, 275). Though the national organization is called the high point of the vocational development, it is recognized that "it will never be easy to attain in centralized form the effective union of all vocational groups" (III, 510).

It is doubly important to set forth as clearly as possible the position of employers and employees in these vocational groups, since they are the two important organized classes of modern society, and because a popular misconception is to view the groups merely as combinations of employer associations and labor unions.[24]

There is no doubt that in his view employer and employees would be in the organization at least on the regional level. Besides the reference given above, other specific statements are:

---

[24] This misunderstanding of the vocational groups is common to both followers and critics of these organizations. An example of a criticism based on this misconception may be seen in Abram L. Harris, *op. cit.*, p. 58: "A corporate reorganization of industry might well begin as a matter of voluntary agreements between some *powerfully organized workers and employers,* just as Pesch supposes." (Italics added.) Though this misconception nullifies the validity of Harris' criticism based on this false notion, he should not be criticized so much as those proponents of vocational groups who have propagated this concept.

Joseph J. Spengler also seems to have this erroneous concept of the vocational groups in mind, when he writes: "Should a corporate type of society succeed contemporary capitalism, upper levels of union officials will be absorbed into the managerial bureaucracy . . ." ("Power Blocs and the Formation and Content of Economic Decisions," *American Economic Review,* XL, Proceedings [May, 1950], p. 428).

The professional-corporative organization and the alliance of the executive labor and the labor which carries out the orders constitutes today in practice a particularly important central point of the moral-organic approach presented by us (IV, 261).

Employers and employees of the same branch belong to the same vocation. They can have differences between themselves, but they may not disrupt the unity of the profession through the class idea and the class struggle. Only in their vocational unity do they become organs of the national economy, are they capable of satisfying the national economic task in the service of the welfare of the whole (III, 239).

It should be observed that to say the employers and employees belong to the same vocational group is not the same as saying that they belong to those groups *qua* employers and *qua* employees. In Congress there are representatives from the east and west, but they are not there precisely and formally as representatives of either seaboard. Nor must employers and employees enter a professional corporation necessarily through a combination of employer and employee organizations.

Elsewhere it is said that the relation between employer and employee from the view of private enterprise is a community of labor with a common interest in the prosperity of the business; from the national economic point of view it is that of a vocational community in the same branch. It is explained: "This (vocational) approach 'meets halfway' the demand for a parallel formation of vocational organizations by employers and employees and offers the one possible foundation of a system of business councils (the democratization of businesses which are not family firms)" (II, 278). This seems to indicate that the corporative order includes more than employers and employees or their organizations. This indication is verified by the explicit statement that "the construction of social organs is naturally not limited to the employers and employees of industry, but in its perfection includes all groups, the whole social body" (II, 224).[25]

Another problem that has aroused considerable interest is what will be the relation between the vocational organizations and the state. As explained above, without the corporative structure the state can exist, but it would not be able to realize its task completely. It is explicitly stated that the state should not by artificial compulsion impose a vocational framework on society; the latter must evolve according to historical conditions (IV, 263, 275; III,387). What type of state is compatible with the corporate order? "Only a genuine state of the people —monarchy or republic— [26] satisfies the social system of labor, not a state which serves the exclusive interest of a ruling class —bourgeoise or proletariat—but such a state which is both a state of rights and welfare, which sees its bounden task in the realization of justice and the public welfare for the benefit of all the people . . ." (II, 241).[27]

In reference to the state a common question is whether the state would be a member of the vocational group. The expecta-

[25] For a confirmation of this interpretation, see Nell-Breuning, "Um die 'Berufsständische Ordnung' " *op. cit.*, pp. 12–13: "Bipartite institutions may in many cases signify a satisfactory improvement over those erected unilaterally. . . . Pioneering, however, must not be confused with the attainment of the goal. If these parallel institutions are made the goal, we thus remain stuck in the dualism of capitalistic class-society, the very thing we seek to overcome."

[26] Cf. II, 263: "*True democracy wishes no part of any discrimination. What it seeks is the life, the development and freedom for every ability in the nation, which serves the good, the welfare of humanity.*" (Italics in original.)

[27] Cf. Joseph A. Schumpeter, "The March into Socialism," *op. cit.*, p. 447: "For instance, a reorganization of society on the lines of the encyclical *Quadragesimo anno,* though presumably possible only in Catholic societies or in societies where the position of the Catholic Church is sufficiently strong, no doubt provides an alternative to socialism that would avoid the 'omnipotent State.' " From the context it is clear that Professor Schumpeter was speaking of the corporate organization described in the encyclical, which is the same as in Pesch. Whether or not a society must be Catholic or one in which the Catholic Church is sufficiently strong before such a reorganization of society is possible may be open to question. At least it would have to be a society which held principles in keeping with Catholic social philosophy.

tion that the state would be is usually based on the assumption that the groups will be composed of employer and employees, so that for the protection of the consumer interest, the state would probably have to be the third member. Nowhere does Pesch say that the state would be a member of the vocational association. Moreover, it seems more in keeping with his general position that the state would not be a member. To mention only the most important considerations, the juridical status of the groups is similar to that of individuals and natural organizations; and the principle of subsidiarity would require that to lesser groups should be left the tasks which they can satisfactorily perform. Also, Pesch looks to the corporative groups to take over some of the functions now performed by the state. The role of the state is the traditional stimulating, protecting, and supplementing. The downfall of the medieval guilds, through their loss of the principle of the common good, shows clearly "how the sharpening of consciences and the vocational order are not sufficient for the regulation of economic life," that there is still required a higher regulating factor, the state, to protect the common welfare from the egoism of individuals and groups (IV, 387). The state remains over the groups, but above and outside of them.

A related question is whether the vocational groups should be free or compulsory organizations. Pesch's position is that there are advantages peculiar to each type, though on balance he favors the free associations. But he states explicitly that compulsory membership in a group is in principle justified (I, 443, note 1). However, he says elsewhere that the application of this principle in concrete circumstances should only be conditional.

> Normally they (compulsory professional associations) may be instituted only for such tasks which the free associations cannot or can only less satisfactorily fulfill, whether it be that according to their nature they are less suitable, or that they

are not sufficiently prepared or are less capable in the economic sphere (III, 504–505).

The free associations are usually more adaptable than the compulsory, which are often restricted by many regulations. The power to recruit and the personal initiative in striving for their goal are more prominent in the free unions. On the other hand, their membership seldom embraces all occupied in a certain segment of the economy; and often they have outside competition. Too, they are more easily perverted into political parties. The advantage of the compulsory union is that it embraces the totality of members in the profession, which makes available a greater income. On the other hand, they are more dependent on the regime which institutes them, and may more easily, on the pretext of an abuse of the power commissioned to them, become the wards of this regime (III, 504).

The main discussion in reference to the vocational groups centers around the important problem, what is their function. In a very general way it can be described as "the ordering of the economy" (IV, 275, note). To be somewhat more specific, this embraces a twofold function: (1) the effective representation of the group's interests before the public and the state; and (2) the regulation, thus the intensification of the powers of the individuals, which in themselves may be deficient (II, 257).

It is the second, the regulatory function, which has given rise to many questions and misunderstandings. Some concept of the nature of this regulation and its scope may be gathered from what has been said in the chapters on consumption, price, and distribution. It is significant that Pesch thinks of this regulation "not as the group's suppression of the individuals and their economic activities but as the elimination of the evils harmful to the vocational group and to the national

community" (IV, 263). Self-regulation by the professions which
protects the members against the arbitrary actions and abuses
by fellow members is considered the supposit of true freedom
(IV, 277–79). In the interest of freedom, self-regulation is
preferred to policing by the state; and also the profession can
better measure the interests of their group (II, ix, 245).

A few examples of particular functions of the vocational
groups are found in the *Lehrbuch*. They should guarantee
the quality of goods offered the consumer. This function, however, may be performed by an independent organization. Also,
the groups will strive for prices fair to the consumer; and they
will be justified in contending against excessive price-cutting.
Another concern will be the abuses in production and distribution of products, including wasteful advertising. An important function will be to cope with the increasing problem
of the concentration of business and monopoly. "The monopolistic exploitation of the people, the oppression of the weaker
enterprises, the injuring of the just interests of the workers
must be prevented" (IV, 554–55). And the first solution is
self-regulation by the profession concerned.

The common objection cited against a vocational order is
that it would create giant monopolies capable of abusing their
power to further their own interests. Pesch, himself, was very
much aware of this danger and frequently warned against it.
"There is no question," admits this ardent solidarist, "that
the associations can be misused to the ruin of the nation and
the group . . ." (II, 257). And he deplores this tendency
which he has observed in modern organizations. "We have
seen in modern society with its division of labor . . . different
vocations, groups striving to be organized, but sadly only too
often, through a disregard of the vocational idea, in associations for special interest" (IV, 263). Three years before his
death he again indicts the postwar corporate organizations
for the same defect.

Up until now the activity of the modern vocational organizations awakens indeed little hope. There is still lacking in the main the correct *weltanschauung* foundation of the concept of the vocation. Therefore the vocational organization up till the present remains more a conglomeration for special interests, a further concession to the materialistic attitude in economic things (V, 788).[28]

What is the solution to the difficulty? Is this a reason not to establish vocational groups? Pesch would answer that this evidences that the state must always be vigilant as the protector of the common good. Also, this danger is a confirmation of Pesch's position as regards the manner of inaugurating such groups. They must not be artificially established by the state, but must grow gradually through a genuine development of the vocational idea; it must be a "grass-roots" movement.

In reference to the broader Peschian solidaristic system of labor of which the vocational order is merely a part, it still cannot be claimed that it will solve all economic and social problems. Its author lays down the general principle: "No system is carried through perfectly" (II, 283). And elsewhere his realism compels him to write:

Still even from the relatively best organization of economic life no paradise can be expected. Considering the weakness of men and the inadequacy of all models, flaws will always arise. The ideal of theory is hardly completely realized, and even the programs of practical economic policy are no magic formulae, even if they move along the proper path (IV, 587).

Perhaps Professor Sumner H. Slichter expressed the feeling and thought of many of his fellow economists when he addressed the American Economic Association:

[28] Cf. J. M. Clark's view of the danger of combining individualism with group organizations, cited above in chapter II, section 5. Basically, the problem of combining individualism with the vocational groups is not different than the combination of this inadequate philosophy with any other group movement, whether it be a trade union or a farm association.

What will happen to the organization of the American economy? Economic institutions are constantly evolving. What comes after capitalism? Is it socialism, a planned economy, or something else?

My vision seems to be poor. I do not see socialism or a planned economy, and yet I know that evolution is steadily occurring. Perhaps the difficulty is that there are several varieties of capitalism and that they are not easily distinguished.[29]

Is the "something else" the solidaristic system of labor? Is this the variety of capitalism towards which we are evolving?

[29] *Op. cit.,* p. 467.

BIBLIOGRAPHY

1. Complete List of the Writings of Heinrich Pesch

a. Books

Pesch, Heinrich. *Christlicher Solidarismus und soziales Arbeitssystem.* Berlin: Deutsche Zentrumspartei, 1922.

—— *Ethik und Volkswirtschaft.* Freiburg im Br.: Herder, 1918.

—— *Lehrbuch der Nationalökonomie.* Volume I: Grundlegung. 4th ed. revised. Freiburg im Br.: Herder, 1924.

—— *Lehrbuch der Nationalökonomie.* Volume II: Allgemeine Volkswirtschaftslehre. I. Volkswirtschaftliche Systeme Wesen und disponierende Ursachen des Volkswohlstandes. 3rd ed. revised. Freiburg im Br.: Herder, 1920.

—— *Lehrbuch der Nationalökonomie.* Volume III: Allgemeine Volkswirtschaftslehre. II. Die aktiven Ursachen im volkswirtschaftlichen Lebensprozesse. 4th ed. revised. Freiburg im Br.: Herder, 1926.

—— *Lehrbuch der Nationalökonomie.* Volume IV: Allgemeine Volkswirtschaftslehre. III. Der volkswirtschaftliche Prozess. 1. Deckung des Volksbedarfs als volkswirtschaftliche Aufgabe. 2. Produktion. Freiburg im Br.: Herder, 1922.

—— *Lehrbuch der Nationalökonomie.* Volume V: Allgemeine Volkswirtschaftslehre. III. Der volkswirtschaftliche Prozess. 3. Tauschverkehr. 4. Einkommens-und Vermögensbildung.

5. Störungen des volkswirtschaftlichen Prozesses. Freiburg im Br.: Herder, 1923.

Pesch, Heinrich. *Liberalismus, Sozialismus und christliche Gesellschaftsordnung.* 2 volumes. 2nd. ed. Freiburg im Br.: Herder, 1901.

—— *Neubau der Gesellschaft.* Freiburg im Br.: Herder, 1919.

—— *Nicht kommunistischer, sondern christlicher Sozialismus.* Berlin: Deutsche Zentrumspartei, 1918.

—— *Die soziale Befähigung der Kirche.* 3rd ed. Berlin: Germania, 1911.

—— *Sozialisierung.* Freiburg im Br.: Herder, 1919.

—— *Die Wohltätigkeitsanstalten der christlichen Barmherzigkeit in Wien.* (Stimmen Ergänzungsheft, 51.) Freiburg im Br.: Herder, 1891.

—— *Ein Wort zum Frieden in der Gewerkschafts-Frage.* Trier: Paulinus, 1908.

b. Contributions to Joint Works

Pesch, Heinrich. "Heinrich Pesch" (autobiography). *Die Volkswirtschaftslehre der Gegenwart in Selbstdarstellungen.* Volume I. Edited by F. Meiner. Leipzig: Meiner, 1924, pp. 190–208.

—— "Nationalismus und Christentum," *Festschrift Felix Porsch zum siebzigsten Geburtstag.* Edited by Görres-Gesellschaft. Paderborn: Schöningh, 1923, pp. 55–58.

—— "Der richtige Weg zur Lösung der sozialen Frage," *Soziale Arbeit im neuen Deutschland; Festschrift zum siebzigsten Geburtstag von Franz Hitze.* M. Gladbach: Volksverein, 1921, pp. 38–60.

—— "Der Solidarismus als Grundprinzip eines organischen Aufbaues der modernen Volkswirtschaft," *Austria Nova.* Edited by "Das neue Österreich." Wien: W. Braumüller, 1916, pp. 56–72.

—— "Staatssozialismus und Privatwirtschaft," *Deutschland und der Katholizismus.* Volume II. Edited by Max Meiner and Herman Sacher. Freiburg im Br.: Herder, 1918, pp. 331–44.

c. Articles

Pesch, Heinrich. "Abhängigkeit der Nationalökonomie von der Moral," *Katholischer Seelsorger,* XIX (1907), Heft 2, pp. 70–83.

—— "Agrarstaat und Industriestaat," *Stimmen aus Maria Laach,* LXI (1901), Heft 4, pp. 345–61; Heft 5, pp. 464–82.

—— "Eine Bankrotterklärung von Seiten des liberalen Ökonomismus," *Stimmen aus Maria Laach,* XLIII (1892), Heft 3, pp. 233–48.

—— "Die Bedingungen des menschlichen Fortschrittes nach Benjamin Kidd," *Stimmen aus Maria Laach,* LI (1896), Heft 4, pp. 341–57; Heft 5, pp. 460–70.

—— "Bevölkerungsprinzip und Bevölkerungsproblem," *Stimmen aus Maria Laach,* LXXV (1908), Heft 3, pp. 281–89.

—— "Die Beziehungen der Nationalökonomie zur Moral und zu den Gesellschaftswissenschaften," *Stimmen aus Maria Laach,* XLVI (1894), Heft 5, pp. 503–18.

—— "Bisheriges und künftiges Verhalten der deutschen Katholiken in der Arbeiterfrage," *Stimmen aus Maria Laach,* LXX (1906), Heft 5, pp. 481–93.

—— "Bodenfrage und Arbeiterinteresse," *Stimmen aus Maria Laach, XCIII* (1917), Heft 3, pp. 279–97.

—— "Christliche Berufsidee und 'kapitalistischer Geist,' " *Stimmen aus Maria Laach,* LXXV (1908), Heft 5, pp. 523–31.

—— "Das christliche-soziale System der Volkswirtschaft," *Stimmen aus Maria Laach,* LXXII (1907), Heft 1, pp. 23–36; Heft 2, pp. 142–60.

—— "Das Coalitionsrecht der Arbeiter," *Stimmen aus Maria Laach,* LIV (1898), Heft 1, pp. 5–17.

—— "Eine neue Ära: unsere wirtschaftlichen Entwicklung," *Stimmen der Zeit,* XC (1915), Heft 3, pp. 243–69.

—— "Eine neue Richtung in der Nationalökonomie," *Stimmen aus Maria Laach,* LXXX (1911), Heft 1, pp. 51–61; Heft 2, pp. 166–82.

—— "Ein neuer Geist im Wirtschaftsleben," *Stimmen der Zeit,* XCII (1917), Heft 4, pp. 418–31.

Pesch, Heinrich. "Freiere Wirtschaft, aber keine Freiwirtschaft," *Stimmen der Zeit*, XCV (1918), Heft 2, pp. 116–31.

—— "Freiwirtschaft oder Wirtschaftsordnung?" *Stimmen aus Maria Laach*, XLIX (1895), Heft 4, pp. 341–59.

—— "Der Gang der wirtschaftsgeschichtlichen Entwicklung," *Stimmen aus Maria Laach*, LXIV (1903), Heft 1, pp. 1–16.

—— "Die geistigen Waffen der Sozialdemokratie," *Stimmen aus Maria Laach*, XL (1891), Heft 4, pp. 373–83; Heft 5, pp. 543–52.

—— "Genossenschaft und Berufsstand," *Stimmen aus Maria Laach*, L (1896), Heft 4, pp. 402–26; Heft 5, pp. 541–58.

—— "Der gerechte Lohn," *Arbeiterwohl*, XV (1895), Heft 1, pp. 78–99.

—— "Geschichte der Bopparder Nachbarschaften und ihrer Kirmesfeirn," *Zeitschrift des Vereins für rheinische und westfälische Volkskunde*, VII (1910), Heft 3, pp. 161–93.

—— "Der Grundirrtum des liberalen Ökonomismus," *Stimmen aus Maria Laach*, XLIII (1892), Heft 2, pp. 113–33.

—— "Die grundlegenden Sätze des marxistischen Sozialismus nach Eduard Bernstein," *Stimmen aus Maria Laach*, LVII (1899), Heft 1, pp. 1–17.

—— "Die Handwerkerfrage der Gegenwart," *Stimmen aus Maria Laach*, LXVIII (1905), Heft 4, pp. 411–20; Heft 5, pp. 531–48.

—— "Henry George und die Enzyklika 'Rerum Novarum,'" *Stimmen aus Maria Laach*, XLVII (1894), Heft 4, pp. 365–82, Heft 5, pp. 523–44.

—— "Die Idee der Gerechtigkeit in den sozialistischen Systemen," *Stimmen aus Maria Laach*, XLIII (1892), Heft 4, pp. 401–12; Heft 5, pp. 465–74.

—— "Imperialismus, Kontinentalismus, Internationalismus," *Stimmen aus Maria Laach*, LXVIII (1910), Heft 1, pp. 67–82.

—— "Kapitalismus," *Stimmen aus Maria Laach*, LXXXVI (1914), Heft 2, pp. 161–74; Heft 3, pp. 273–86; Heft 4, pp. 412–20; Heft 5, pp. 528–88.

—— "Die katholische Caritas und ihre Gegner," *Stimmen aus Maria Laach*, LXXVI (1909), Heft 5, pp. 511–12.

Pesch, Heinrich. "Die katholische Kirche in ihrem Verhältnis zur Kultur und Civilisation," *Stimmen aus Maria Laach,* XLVIII (1895), Heft 1, pp. 1–11; Heft 2, pp. 178–90.

—— "Der Katholicismus: die Religion der 'Weltflucht,' " *Stimmen aus Maria Laach,* LVI (1899), Heft 1, pp. 1–14.

—— "Kennzeichen des Volkswohlstandes," *Stimmen aus Maria Laach,* LXXIII (1907), Heft 1, pp. 24–42, Heft 2, pp. 179–200.

—— "Kirche und Kapitalismus," *Stimmen aus Maria Laach,* LXV (1903), Heft 1, pp. 114–16.

—— "Kirchliche Autorität und wirtschaftliche Organisation," *Stimmen aus Maria Laach,* LXXV (1908), Heft 4, pp. 410–24.

—— "Krieg und Volkswirtschaft," *Stimmen der Zeit,* LXXXVIII (1915), Heft 2, pp. 122–47; Heft 3, pp. 220–31.

—— "Krieg und Wirtschaftsleben," *Stimmen der Zeit,* LXXXIX (1915), Heft 4, pp. 322–59; Heft 5, pp. 440–62.

—— "Kultur, Fortschritt, Reform," *Stimmen aus Maria Laach,* LXXIV (1908), Heft 5, pp. 473–86.

—— "Lehrlingsvereine und Lehrlingsasyle," *Stimmen aus Maria Laach,* XL (1891), Heft 3, pp. 313–19.

—— "Die Lohnfrage in der Praxis," *Stimmen aus Maria Laach,* LIII (1897), Heft 3, pp. 225–39.

—— "Lohnvertrag und gerechter Lohn," *Stimmen aus Maria Laach,* LII (1897), Heft 1, pp. 22–30; Heft 2, pp. 128–43; Heft 3, pp. 253–67; Heft 4, pp. 373–89.

—— "Die marxistische Theorie der modernen Gesellschaft und ihrer Entwicklung im Lichte der Bernsteinschen Kritik," *Stimmen aus Maria Laach,* LVII (1899), Heft 2, pp. 105–22; Heft 3, pp. 225–47.

—— "Die Methoden der Volkswirtschaftslehre," *Stimmen aus Maria Laach,* XLIX (1895), Heft 5, pp. 449–61.

—— "Die Naturgesetze der kulturellen Entwicklung und die Volkswirtschaft," *Stimmen aus Maria Laach,* LI (1896), Heft 1, pp. 1–20; Heft 2, pp. 156–74.

—— "Die 'natürliche Ordnung' im physiokratischen System," *Stimmen aus Maria Laach,* LV (1898), Heft 1, pp. 44–56.

Pesch, Heinrich. "Neuere Publikationen über den marxistischen Sozialismus," *Stimmen aus Maria Laach*, LVIII (1900), Heft 4, pp. 349–61; Heft 5, pp. 520–35.

——— "Die neuzeitliche Entwicklung im Handwerk," *Stimmen aus Maria Laach*, LXVII (1904), Heft 5, pp. 486–504.

——— "Öffentliche Betriebe und Monopole," *Stimmen aus Maria Laach*, LXXXV (1913), Heft 1, pp. 14–30.

——— "Die ökonomischen Lehren des Marx'schen Sozialismus," *Stimmen aus Maria Laach*, XLI (1891), Heft 1, pp. 23–58.

——— "Die Pflicht im Wirtschaftsleben," *Stimmen aus Maria Laach*, LX (1901), Heft 1, pp. 16–30.

——— "Pflichten und Schranken des Eigenthums," *Stimmen aus Maria Laach*, XLIX (1895), Heft 1, pp. 16–32.

——— "Die Philosophie des 'wissenschaftlichen' Sozialismus," *Stimmen aus Maria Laach*, XLI (1891), Heft 3, pp. 245–65; Heft 4, pp. 357–79.

——— "Das Privateigenthum am Grund und Boden im Mittelalter," *Stimmen aus Maria Laach*, XLV (1893), Heft 3, pp. 264–77; Heft 4, pp. 345–55.

——— "Produktivität der Volkswirtschaft und volkswirtschaftliche Produktivität," *Archiv für Rechts-und Wirtschaftsphilosophie*, IX, Heft 2, pp. 225–34; Heft 3, pp. 321–32.

——— "Reform des Wohnungswesens," *Stimmen aus Maria Laach*, LXV (1903), Heft 3, pp. 251–73.

——— "Segensreiches Wirken des Volksvereins," *Stimmen aus Maria Laach*, LXXII (1907), Heft 3, pp. 359–60.

——— "Soziale Gegensätze und deren Versöhnung," *Stimmen aus Maria Laach*, XXXIX (1890), Heft 3, pp. 270–81; Heft 4, pp. 352–74.

——— "Solidarismus," *Stimmen aus Maria Laach*, LXIII (1902), Heft 1, pp. 38–60; Heft 3, pp. 307–24.

——— "Sozialdemokratie und Gewerkschaft," *Stimmen aus Maria Laach*, LVIII (1900), Heft 1, pp. 29–41.

——— "Die sozialen Klassen," *Stimmen aus Maria Laach*, LXXIV (1908), Heft 4, pp. 394–406; Heft 5, pp. 519–31.

——— "Der Staatssozialismus," *Stimmen aus Maria Laach*, XLVI (1894), Heft 1, pp. 1–14; Heft 3, pp. 269–75.

Pesch, Heinrich. "Streik und Lockout," *Stimmen aus Maria Laach*, LXXVII (1909), Heft 1, pp. 1–12.

—— "Das Sweating-System in England," *Stimmen aus Maria Laach*, LII (1897), Heft 4, pp. 471–74.

—— "Die theoretischen Voraussetzungen der klassischen Nationalökonomie," *Stimmen aus Maria Laach*, XLII (1892), Heft 4, pp. 373–404.

—— "Ursachen des wirtschaftlichen Niederganges katholischer Völker," *Stimmen aus Maria Laach*, XLVIII (1895), Heft 4, pp. 361–71.

—— "Die Volkswirtschaft der Zukunft," *Stimmen der Zeit*, XCII (1917), Heft 5, pp. 495–518.

—— "Volkswirtschaftliche Aufgabe und Weltwirtschaft," *Weltwirtschaftliches Archiv*, VI (1915), Heft 1, pp. 21–40.

—— "Volkswirtschaftliche Harmonien," *Stimmen der Zeit*, XCII (1917), Heft 6, pp. 654–79.

—— "Vor Sonnenaufgang?" *Stimmen der Zeit*, XCIX (1920), Heft 3, pp. 204–16.

—— "Wandlungen in der volkswirtschaftlichen Organisation," *Stimmen aus Maria Laach*, LXXXI (1911), Heft 4, pp. 373–87; Heft 5, pp. 523–34.

—— "Wechsel und Wandel in der Handwerkerpolitik," *Stimmen aus Maria Laach*, LXVI (1904), Heft 1, pp. 62–83; Heft 2, pp. 186–99.

—— "Weltwirtschaftliche Tendenzen und volkswirtschaftliche Politik," *Stimmen aus Maria Laach*, LXII (1902), Heft 1, pp. 18–32.

—— "Die Wohnungsfrage in ihren Ursachen," *Stimmen aus Maria Laach*, LXIV (1903), Heft 5, pp. 524–44.

—— "Ziele und Grenzen der staatlichen Wirtschaftspolitik," *Stimmen aus Maria Laach*, L (1896), Heft 1, pp. 1–10; Heft 2, pp. 180–90.

—— "Zinsgrund und Zinsgrenze," *Zeitschrift für katholische Theologie*, XII (1888), Heft 1, pp. 36–74; Heft 3, pp. 393–418.

—— "Zur Bevölkerungsfrage," *Stimmen aus Maria Laach*, XLVII (1894), Heft 1, pp. 1–24.

Pesch, Heinrich. "Zur Frage der börsenmässigen Terminhandels mit landwirtschaftlichen Produkten," *Stimmen aus Maria Laach,* LX (1901), Heft 4, pp. 349–67.

—— "Zur Geschichte der sozialistischen Bewegung in Deutschland," *Stimmen aus Maria Laach,* XLIV (1893), Heft 1, pp. 13–23; Heft 3, pp. 285–95; XLV (1893), Heft 1, pp. 13–24; Heft 2, pp. 105–23.

—— "Zur katholisch-sozialen Bewegung in der Schweiz," *Stimmen aus Maria Laach,* LIV (1898), Heft 4, pp. 361–75; Heft 5, pp. 477–92.

—— "Der Zusammenbruch der heutigen Gesellschaft," *Stimmen aus Maria Laach,* XLII (1892), Heft 1, pp. 14–25.

d. Review Articles

Pesch, Heinrich. "*Cours d'Economie sociale* [by] C. Antoine," *Stimmen aus Maria Laach,* LII (1897), Heft 3, pp. 325–28.

—— "*Staatslexikon* [by] J. Bachem," *Stimmen aus Maria Laach,* LXVII (1904), Heft 5, pp. 557–61.

—— "*Die Getreidepolitik der Päpste* [by] U. Benigni und R. Birner," *Stimmen aus Maria Laach,* LVI (1899), Heft 5, p. 561.

—— "*Die soziale Frage* [by] J. Biederlack," *Stimmen aus Maria Laach,* LV (1898), Heft 3, pp. 329–30.

—— "*Erbrecht und ländliche Erbsitten in Frankreich* [by] V. Brandt," *Stimmen aus Maria Laach,* LXI (1901), Heft 1, pp. 79–84.

—— "*Die katholischen Wohltätigkeits-Anstalten und-Vereine, sowie das katholisch-soziale Vereinswesen insbesondere in der Erzdiöcese Köln* [by] M. Brandts," *Stimmen aus Maria Laach,* LI (1896), Heft 1, pp. 105–10.

—— "*La solidarite sociale comme principe des lois* [by] C. Brunot," *Stimmen aus Maria Laach,* LXVII (1904), Heft 3, pp. 327–29.

—— "*Le Socialisme et le Droit de Propriete* [by] A. Castelein," *Stimmen aus Maria Laach,* LIII (1897), Heft 4, pp. 436–37.

—— "*Die katholische Moral in ihren Voraussehungen und*

ihren Grundlinien [by] V. Cathrein," *Stimmen aus Maria Laach*, LXXII (1907), Heft 5, pp. 552–54.

Pesch, Heinrich. *"La solidarite sociale, ses nouvelles formules* [by] E. d'Eichtal," *Stimmen aus Maria Laach*, LXVII (1904), Heft 3, pp. 327–28.

—— *"Kleine Schriften zur Zeitgeschichte und Politik* [by] G. von Hertling," *Stimmen aus Maria Laach*, LIV (1898), Heft 4, pp. 450–53.

—— *"Die Agrarfrage der Gegenwart* (4te Abteilung) [by] C. Jäger," *Stimmen aus Maria Laach*, XLIX (1895), Heft 4, pp. 427–29.

—— *"Die bayrische Steuer-Reform von 1899* [by] C. Jäger," *Stimmen aus Maria Laach*, LVIII (1900), Heft 5, pp. 563–69.

—— *"Die sozialen Lehren des Freiherrn Karl von Vogelsang* [by] W. Klopp," *Stimmen aus Maria Laach*, XLIX (1895), Heft 2, pp. 207–10.

—— *"Arbeiterausschüsse* [by] H. Koch," *Stimmen aus Maria Laach*, LXXII (1907), Heft 3, pp. 328–29.

—— *"Konfessionsstatistik Deutschlands* [by] H. A. Krose," *Stimmen aus Maria Laach*, LXVII (1904), Heft 4, pp. 438–39.

—— *"V. A. Hubers ausgewählte Schriften über Sozialreform und Genossenschaftswesen* [by] K. Munding," *Stimmen aus Maria Laach*, L (1896), Heft 3, pp. 333–38.

—— *"Jesus Christus und die soziale Frage* [by] F. G. Peabody and E. Müllenhoff," *Stimmen aus Maria Laach*, LXV (1903), Heft 4, pp. 464–65.

—— *"Soziale und politische Zeitfragen* (Volume I: Der Antrag Kanitz [by] F. Pichler; Volume II: Das Gesetz zur Bekämpfung des unlautern Wettbewerbes [by] H. Roeren)," *Stimmen aus Maria Laach*, III (1897), Heft 2, pp. 212–16.

—— *"M. Fassbender* [by] F. W. Raisseisen," *Stimmen aus Maria Laach*, LXIV (1903), Heft 3, pp. 459–62.

—— *"Die Eigenthumslehre nach Thomas von Aquin und dem modernen Sozialismus* [by] F. Schauf," *Stimmen aus Maria Laach*, LVI (1899), Heft 3, pp. 341–42.

Pesch, Heinrich. "*Das Buch vom gerechten Richter* [by] D. Spielberg," *Stimmen aus Maria Laach*, LXV (1903), Heft 5, p. 579.

—— "*Manuel Social* [by] A. Vermeersch," *Stimmen aus Maria Laach*, LXVII (1904), Heft 4, pp. 439–40.

—— "*Quaestiones de justitia* [by] A. Vermeersch," *Stimmen aus Maria Laach*, LXII (1902), Heft 3, pp. 339–40.

—— "*Sozialpolitik und Moral* [by] F. Walter," *Stimmen aus Maria Laach*, LVI (1899), Heft 4, pp. 457–59.

—— "*Didaktik als Bildungslehre nach ihren Beziehungen zur Sozialforschung und zur Geschichte der Bildung* [by] O. Willmann," *Stimmen aus Maria Laach*, XLI (1891), Heft 2, pp. 204–11.

e. Newspaper Articles

Pesch, Heinrich. "Christlicher Solidarismus," *Germania*, September 28, 1921, pp. 1–2.

—— "Volkswirtschaft der Zukunft," *Germania*, December 14, 1918, pp. 1, 2, 3.

—— "Zum Gewerkschaftstreit," *Kölnische Volkszeitung*, November 4, 1908, p. 1.

—— "Gewerkschaftstreit," *Kölnische Volkszeitung*, November 16, 1908, p. 1.

2. *Other Works Cited*

a. Books

Bergson, Abram. "Socialist Economics," *A Survey of Contemporary Economics*. Edited by Howard S. Ellis. Philadelphia: Blakiston, 1948, pp. 412–48.

Bober, Mandell M. "Economic Assumptions and Monopoly," *Explorations in* Economics. New York: McGraw-Hill, 1936, pp. 336–45.

Boulding, Kenneth E. *A Reconstruction of Economics*. New York: Wiley, 1950.

Bye, Raymond T. *Social Economy and the Price System.* New York: Macmillan, 1950.

Clark, John M. *Alternative to Serfdom.* New York: Knopf, 1948.

—— "Financing High-Level Employment," *Financing American Prosperity.* Edited by Paul T. Homan and Fritz Machlup. New York: Twentieth Century Fund, 1945, pp. 71–125.

Dempsey, Bernard W. *Interest and Usury.* London: Dobson, 1948.

Ellis, Howard S. "Economic Expansion Through Competitive Markets," *Financing American Prosperity.* Edited by Paul T. Homan and Fritz Machlup. New York: Twentieth Century Fund, 1945, pp. 126–98.

Fellner, William. *Competition Among the Few.* New York: Knopf, 1949.

—— and Bernard F. Haley. "Introduction" to *Readings in the Theory of Income Distribution.* Selected by William Fellner and Bernard F. Haley. Philadelphia: Blakiston, 1946, pp. vii–xii.

Flubacher, Joseph F. *The Concept of Ethics in the History of Economics.* New York: Vantage, 1950.

Fraser, Lindley M. *Economic Thought and Language: A Critique of Some Fundamental Economic Concepts.* London: A. & C. Black, 1947.

Galbraith, J. K. "Monopoly and the Concentration of Economic Power," *A Survey of Contemporary Economics.* Edited by Howard S. Ellis. Philadelphia: Blakiston, 1948, pp. 99–128.

Gordon, Robert A. "Enterprise, Profits, and the Modern Corporation," *Explorations in Economics.* New York: McGraw-Hill, 1936, pp. 306–16. Also in *Readings in the Theory of Income Distribution.* Selected by William Fellner and Bernard F. Haley. Philadelphia: Blakiston, 1946, pp. 558–70.

Haley, Bernard F. "Value and Distribution," *A Survey of Contemporary Economics.* Edited by Howard S. Ellis. Philadelphia: Blakiston, 1948, pp. 1–48.

Keynes, John M. *General Theory of Employment, Interest and Money.* New York: Harcourt Brace, 1936.

Keynes, John N. *Scope and Method of Political Economy.* 4th ed. London: Macmillan, 1930.

Knight, Frank H. *Risk, Uncertainty, and Profit.* Boston: Houghton Mifflin, 1921.

Lange, Oscar. "On the Economic Theory of Socialism," *On the Economic Theory of Socialism.* Edited by B. Lippincott. Minneapolis: Minnesota, 1948, pp. 55–143.

Lechtape, Heinrich. *Die Frage der Steuergerechtigkeit.* (Grundsätzliches zur Finanzreform auf Grund des Solidaritätssystems von Heinrich Pesch, S.J.). Freiburg im Br.: Herder, 1920.

Marshall, Alfred. *Principles of Economics.* 8th ed. London: Macmillan, 1936.

Moulton, Harold. *Controlling Factors in Economic Development.* Washington, D.C.: Brookings, 1949.

Mueller, Franz H. *Heinrich Pesch and His Theory of Solidarism.* St. Paul, Minnesota: College of St. Thomas, 1941.

Nell-Breuning, Oswald von. *Die soziale Enzyklika.* Cologne: Katholischer Tat-Verlag, 1932. English edition, *Reorganization of Social Economy.* Edited by B. W. Dempsey. New York: Bruce, 1936.

Polanyi, Karl. *The Great Transformation.* New York: Rinehart, 1944.

Robbins, Lionel. *An Essay on the Nature and Significance of Economic Science.* 2nd ed. revised and extended. London: Macmillan, 1948.

v. Schäffle, Albert. *Die Quintessenz des Sozialismus.* 7th ed. Gotha: F. A. Perthes, 1879.

Schumpeter, Joseph A. *Capitalism, Socialism, and Democracy.* 2nd ed. New York: Harper, 1947.

Shoup, Carl S. "Development and Use of National Income Data," *A Survey of Contemporary Economics.* Edited by Howard S. Ellis. Philadelphia: Blakiston, 1948, pp. 288–313.

Stigler, George F. *The Theory of Competitive Price*. New York: Macmillan, 1942.

Stolper, Gustav. *German Economy, 1870–1940*. New York: Reynal & Hitchcock, 1940.

Walker, E. Ronald. *From Economic Theory to Policy*. Chicago: Chicago Press, 1943.

Wright, David McCord "Prospects for Capitalism," *A Survey of Contemporary Economics*. Edited by Howard S. Ellis. Philadelphia: Blakiston, 1948, pp. 449–72.

b. Articles

American Economic Association. "On Teaching Undergraduate Economics," *American Economic Review*, XL (December, 1950), Supplement, pp. 1–17.

Bladen, Vincent W. "John Stuart Mill's *Principles:* A Centenary Estimate," *American Economic Review*, XXXIX (May, 1949), Proceedings, pp. 1–12.

Bloom, Gordon F. "A Reconsideration of the Theory of Exploitation," *Quarterly Journal of Economics*, LV (1940–1941), pp. 413–42. Also in *Readings in the Theory of Income Distribution*. Selected by William Fellner and Bernard F. Haley. Philadelphia: Blakiston, 1946, pp. 245–77.

Bober, Mandell M. "The Sociology and Economics of Class Conflict" (Discussion), *American Economic Review*, XXXIX (May, 1949), Proceedings, pp. 37–46.

Boulding, Kenneth E. "The Consumption Concept in Economic Theory," *American Economic Review*, XXXV (May, 1945), Proceedings, pp. 1–14.

—— "Professor Tarshis and the State of Economics," *American Economic Review*, XXXVIII (March, 1948), pp. 92–102.

—— "Recent Anti-Trust Decisions" (Discussion), *American Economic Review*, XXXIX (May, 1949), Proceedings, pp. 311–21.

Briefs, Goetz. "Heinrich Pesch," *Encyclopedia of the Social Sciences*, XII (1937), pp. 91–92.

Briefs, Goetz. "Pesch and His Contemporaries," *Social Order,* I (April, 1951), pp. 153–60.

Buchanan, Daniel. "The Historical Approach to Rent and Price Theory," *Economica,* IX (June, 1929), pp. 123–55. Also in *Readings in the Theory of Income Distribution.* Selected by William Fellner and Bernard F. Haley. Philadelphia: Blakiston, 1946, pp. 599–637.

Bye, Raymond T. "The Scope and Definition of Economics," *Journal of Political Economy,* XLVII (October, 1939), pp. 623–47.

—— "Some Criteria of Social Economy," *American Economic Review,* XXXIV (March, 1944), Proceedings, pp. 1–8.

Cannan, Edwin. " '*An Essay on the Nature and Significance of Economic Science*' by Lionel Robbins" (Review), *Economic Journal,* XLII (September, 1932), pp. 424–27.

Chamberlin, E. H. "Product Heterogeneity and Public Policy," *American Economic Review,* XL (May, 1950), Proceedings, pp. 85–92.

Clark, John M. "Distribution," *Encyclopedia of the Social Sciences,* V (1931), pp. 167–73. Also in *Readings in the Theory of Income Distribution.* Selected by William Fellner and Bernard F. Haley. Philadelphia: Blakiston, 1946, pp. 58–71.

—— "Economic Means—To What Ends?" *American Economic Review,* XL (December, 1950), Supplement, pp. 34–51.

—— "Educational Functions of Economics after the War," *American Economic Review,* XXXIV (March, 1944), Proceedings, pp. 58–78.

—— "Some Current Cleavages Among Economists," *American Economic Review,* XXXVII (May, 1947), Proceedings, pp. 1–11.

—— "Toward a Concept of Workable Competition," *American Economic Review,* XXX (June, 1940), pp. 241–56. Also in *Readings in the Social Control of Industry.* Selected by Edgar M. Hoover, Jr., and Joel Dean. Philadelphia: Blakiston, 1942, pp. 452–75.

Enke, Stephen. "On Maximizing Profits: A Distinction Between Chamberlin and Robinson," *American Economic Review*, XLI (September, 1951), pp. 566–78.

Ellis, Howard S. "The Economic Way of Thinking," *American Economic Review*, XL (March, 1950), pp. 1–12.

—— "Research as Seen in *A Survey of Contemporary Economics*," *American Economic Review*, XXXIX (May, 1949), Proceedings, pp. 427–39.

Fraser, Lindley M. "How Do We Want Economists to Behave?", *Economic Journal*, XLII (December, 1932), pp. 555–70.

Graham, Frank D. "Ethics in the Study of Democratic Principles" (Discussion), *American Economic Review*, XXXIV (March, 1944), Proceedings, pp. 48–57.

Gundlach, Gustav. "Solidarist Economics," *Social Order*, I (April, 1951), pp. 181–85.

Harris, Abram L. "The Scholastic Revival: The Economics of Heinrich Pesch," *Journal of Political Economy*, LIV (February, 1946), pp. 38–59.

Hawtrey, R. G. "The Need for Faith," *Economic Journal*, LVI (September, 1946), pp. 351–65.

Hicks, J. R. "The Foundations of Welfare Economics," *Economic Journal*, XLIX (December, 1939), pp. 696–712.

Keirstead, B. S. "The Conditions of Survival," *American Economic Review*, XL (May, 1950), Proceedings, pp. 435–45.

Keynes, John M. "Savings and Usury," *Economic Journal*, XLII (March, 1932), pp. 123–37.

Knight, Frank H. "The Nature of Economic Science in Some Recent Discussion," *American Economic Review*, XXIV (June, 1934), pp. 225–38.

Kyrk, Hazel. "The Income Distribution as a Measure of Economic Welfare," *American Economic Review*, XL (May, 1950), Proceedings, pp. 342–55.

Lechtape, Heinrich. "Heinrich Pesch," *Staatslexikon*, IV (1931), col. 132–35.

Marchal, Jean. "The Construction of a New Theory of Profit," *American Economic Review*, XLI (September, 1951), pp. 549–65.

Mitchell, Wesley C. "Ethics in the Study of Democratic Politics"

(Discussion), *American Economic Review,* XXXIV (March, 1944), Proceedings, pp. 48–57.

Moos, S. "Laissez-faire, Planning and Ethics," *Economic Journal,* LV (April, 1945), pp. 17–27.

Mueller, Franz. "I Knew Heinrich Pesch," *Social Order,* I (April, 1951), pp. 147–52.

Mulcahy, Richard E. "Economic Freedom in Heinrich Pesch," *Social Order,* I (April, 1951), pp. 161–68.

—— "The Welfare Economics of Heinrich Pesch," *Quarterly Journal of Economics,* LXIII (August, 1949), pp. 342–60.

v. Nell-Breuning, Oswald. "Berufsständische Ordnung," *Stimmen der Zeit,* CXLIII (1949), Heft 4, pp. 254–61.

—— "The Concept of a Just Price," *Review of Social Economy,* VIII (September, 1950), pp. 111–28.

—— "Lohn, Lohngerechtigkeit," *Wörterbuch der Politik,* III: *Zur Sozialen Frage* (1949), cols. 143–54.

—— "The Peschian Interest Theory," *Social Order,* I (April, 1951), pp. 177–80.

—— "Um die 'Berufsständische Ordnung,'" *Stimmen der Zeit,* CXLII (1948), Heft 7, pp. 6–19.

—— "Verbrauch," *Wörterbuch der Politik,* IV: *Zur Wirtschaftsordnung* (1949), cols. 115–20.

Nickel, K. E. "Literaturberichte," *Volkswirtschaftliche Blätter,* XXVIII (1929), Heft 1, pp. 53–56.

Nussbaum, F. L. "The Economic History of Renaissance Europe," *Journal of Modern History,* XIII (December, 1941), pp. 527–45.

Parsons, T. "Reply to Professor Knight," *Canadian Journal of Economics and Political Science,* VI (August, 1940), pp. 466–72.

Pigou, A. C. "Some Aspects of Welfare Economics," *American Economic Review,* XLI (June, 1951), pp. 287–302.

Reynolds, Lloyd G. "Relations Between Wage Rates, Costs and Prices," *American Economic Review,* XXXII (March, 1942), Proceedings, pp. 275–89. Also in *Readings in the*

Theory of Income Distribution. Selected by William Fellner and Bernard F. Haley. Philadelphia: Blakiston, 1946, pp. 294–313.

Robbins, Lionel. "Interpersonal Comparisons of Utility," *Economic Journal,* XLVIII (December, 1938), pp. 635–41.

—— "Live and Dead Issues in the Methodology of Economics," *Economica,* V (August, 1938), new series, pp. 342–52.

Sacher, Hermann. "Schrifttum zur christlichen Gessellschaftslehre und zur Sozialen Frage," *Wörterbuch der Politik,* III: *Zur Sozialen Frage* (1949), cols. 202–34.

Salz, Arthur. "The Present Position of Economics," *American Economic Review,* XXXIV (March, 1944), Proceedings, pp. 15–24.

Schumpeter, Joseph A. "The March into Socialism," *American Economic Review,* XL (May, 1950), Proceedings, pp. 445–56.

Slichter, Sumner H. "Long Term Economic Trends," *American Economic Review,* XL (May, 1950), pp. 457–69.

Spengler, Joseph J. "Power Blocs and the Formation and Content of Economic Decisions," *American Economic Review,* XL (May, 1950), Proceedings, pp. 413–30.

Suranyi-Unger, Theo. "Facts and Ends in Economics," *Economic Journal,* XLIX (March, 1939), pp. 1–13.

Wallace, Donald H. "Monopolistic Competition and Public Policy," *American Economic Review,* XXVI (March, 1936), Proceedings, pp. 77–87. Also in *Readings in the Social Control of Industry.* Selected by Edgar M. Hoover, Jr., and Joel Dean. Philadelphia: Blakiston, 1942, pp. 263–79.

Williamson, Harold F. "An Appraisal of American Economic Progress," *American Economic Review,* XL (May, 1950), Proceedings, pp. 107–17.

Wolfe, Albert B. "Economy and Democracy," *American Economic Review,* XXXIV (March, 1944), pp. 1–20.

—— "Undergraduate Teaching of Economics" (Discussion), *American Economic Review,* XXXVI (May, 1946), Proceedings, pp. 848–52.

Wright, David McCord. "The Economics of a Classless Society," *American Economic Review*, XXXIX (May, 1949), Proceedings, pp. 27–36.

Yenni, Jacques. "Pesch's Goal of the Economy," *Social Order*, I (April, 1951), pp. 169–76.

INDEX